Series / Number 07-002

OPERATIONS RESEARCH METHODS: As Applied to Political Science and the Legal Process

STUART S. NAGEL
with **MARIAN NEEF**

University of Illinois

SAGE PUBLICATIONS
The International Professional Publishers
Newbury Park London New Delhi

For information address:

SAGE Publications, Inc.
2455 Teller Road
Newbury Park, California 91320

SAGE Publications Ltd.
6 Bonhill Street
London EC2A 4PU
United Kingdom

SAGE Publications India Pvt. Ltd.
M-32 Market
Greater Kailash I
New Delhi 110 048 India

International Standard Book Number 0-8039-0651-X

Library of Congress Catalog Card No. L.C. 76-25693

95 96 15 14 13

When citing a University Paper, please use the proper form. Remember to cite the correct Sage University Paper series title and include the paper number. One of the two following formats can be adapted (depending on the style manual used):

(1) IVERSEN, GUDMUND R. and NORPOTH, HELMUT (1976) "Analysis of Variance." Sage University Paper series on Quantitative Applications in the Social Sciences, 07-001. Beverly Hills and London: Sage Pubns.

OR

(2) Iversen, Gudmund R. and Norpoth, Helmut. 1976. *Analysis of Variance.* Sage University Paper series on Quantitative Applications in the Social Sciences, series no. 07-001. Beverly Hills and London: Sage Publications.

CONTENTS

Editor's Introduction

OPERATIONS RESEARCH was born in the late thirties with the German air attack on Britain and the urgent need to incorporate radar into the tactics of British air defense. Small teams of scientists, gathered from various disciplines to cope with that immediate crisis, then turned their expertise to other problems and the use of such OPERATIONS RESEARCH teams became widespread—increased by several orders of magnitude with the development of computers as a team tool.

Today it is unrealistic to attempt to pinpoint the applications of OPERATIONS RESEARCH. It has become a basic component of most industrial, military, and academic organizations. It can best be defined by its three inherent characteristics: its systems, its use of interdisciplinary teams, and its methodology—linear programming, inventory modeling, and decision theory.

All three techniques are explored in this paper, with the emphasis on the central OPERATIONS RESEARCH METHOD: linear programming. As this paper demonstrates, linear programming is an accessible and comprehensible methodology, requiring only an elementary facility with mathematics. It is not per se a statistical technique, although it includes some assumptions that are similar to statistical procedures. It allows a researcher to answer this question:

What is the highest (or lowest) possible value for a variable? (Presuming that he has a set of other variables that are assumed to determine the level of the first variable, and also presuming that he has a set of constraints that affect either set of variables.)

For example: How can a cafeteria maximize the amount of protein (highest value) or minimize the amount of carbohydrate (lowest value) served on its lunch menu? Using the first part of the question, the *variables* that affect the maximizing of protein include the quantity of protein in the foods available from suppliers and the consumers' choices of higher protein selections from the menu. The *constraints* include (1) the total amount of protein in foods available to the cafeteria and (2) the cost limitations of high-protein foods that the cafeteria can obtain while remaining within its budget and retaining a profit margin. The only *assumptions* needed are that the relationship between the optimal amount of protein and the two determining variables is linear and that the constraints are not mutually contradictory or otherwise impossible. This possibility can usually be avoided by sufficient care in constructing the problem. If this is not possible, valuable information can be obtained in discovering that the problem (as defined) has no solution.

In this paper, OPERATIONS RESEARCH METHODS are applied not to cafeterias but to races for congressional seats, assessments of campaign dollars to media, and several policy problems in the area of public law and criminal justice: for example, what is the optimum level of free press and fair trial? This study suggests only a few of the potential applications of this versatile technique. For example, OPERATIONS RESEARCH METHODS are particularly popular with economists who attempt to maximize the output of a firm, given its resources for producing goods and the available level of technology. Constraints here include the market demand for the firm's products, the capacity of workers to produce, and a general restriction that profits tend to increase with output.

While OPERATIONS RESEARCH METHODS have not yet been used extensively throughout the fields of psychology, education, and sociology, some researchers and practitioners have been using these techniques for many years (in industrial psychology, for example). In the future, the legal problems discussed in this paper may suggest further exploration by sociologists using these techniques. Educators and psychologists will find invaluable a variant of linear programming in which the problem is to "find the right person for each job"—that is, to maximize efficient use of manpower from a pool of applicants for a set of available jobs or classrooms. Each applicant is given a qualification score for each vacancy; the constraints may establish that all vacancies be filled, that each qualified applicant receive a position, that equal opportunities be provided for minority candidates, or whatever preconditions are desired. The same model has been occasionally borrowed by political scientists; for example, some political researchers have used it to assign freshmen members of congress to committee vacancies.*

Other applications of these techniques can be established whenever explicit criteria and constraints can be established and OPERATIONS RESEARCH METHODS employed—wherever there are such problems in need of solution.

—E. M. Uslaner, Series Editor

*Readers who are interested in this application may consult the paper written by the series editor: Eric M. Uslaner (1974) *Congressional Committee Assignments: Alternative Models for Behavior.* Sage Professional Papers in American Politics, vol. 2, series no. 04-019. Beverly Hills and London: Sage Publications.

OPERATIONS RESEARCH METHODS: As Applied to Political Science and the Legal Process

STUART NAGEL
MARIAN NEEF
University of Illinois

I. BASIC CONCEPTS AND EXAMPLES

Operations research is the study of the application of mathematical techniques to the choosing among various alternatives that decision or decisions that will maximize some quantitatively measured goal. The purpose of this paper is to discuss the three most commonly used operations research methods as they apply to social science in general and to political science and the legal process in particular. Those three methods are linear programming, inventory modeling, and decision theory, with linear programming being especially central in operations research.

Linear programming or linear optimizing can be defined as a geometric or algebraic procedure whereby one finds the optimum allocation of something between two or more alternatives in light of certain goals and in light of given constraints or conditions. The emphasis here is on the notion of

AUTHORS' NOTE: *The authors thank Barry Chafetz, Tony Champagne, Thomas Eimermann, Kathleen Reinbolt, and Paul Wice for their participation in the applications which are used in this paper while they were graduate students at the University of Illinois. Thanks are also owed to the Ford Foundation Public Policy Committee, the LEAA National Institute, and the University of Illinois Law and Society Program for financing various aspects of this research. The paper itself is partly based on a study presented at the 1975 annual meeting of the American Political Science Association under the title "Policy Optimizing Models: Applied to Political Science and the Legal Process."*

optimum allocation or optimum mix. Linear programming can be approached in its simplest form from the perspective of choosing among two activities, each of which bears a linear relationship with the goal to be achieved. The relationship is linear in the sense that as the activities increase or decrease the degree of goal achievement increases or decreases proportionately rather than at an increasing or decreasing rate. After discussing this relatively simple situation, we will then discuss the multiple activity situation and the nonlinear situation.

Inventory modeling can be defined as a geometric or algebraic procedure whereby one finds the optimum quantity or optimum inventory in a situation where doing either too much or too little will result in excessive costs or unduly low benefits. The emphasis here is on the notion of optimum level. Determining the optimum level on a policy variable will first be approached where a constrained linear relation is involved such that the more the policy is adopted, the more the goal is achieved. However, a policy level usually cannot be continuously increased in view of the presence of political, legal, economic, or other constraints. After discussing this relatively simple situation, we will then discuss the nonlinear optimum level problem.

Decision theory can be defined as a geometric or algebraic procedure whereby one chooses among alternatives in order to maximize given goals in light of probabilistic or uncertain events. The emphasis here is on the notion of optimum choice under uncertainty or risk. Decision theory can involve a one-person decision situation or a two-person or two-group bargaining situation in which each side may be faced with a separate decision theory problem. The two-person bargaining situation lends itself especially well to illustrating how an optimum dynamic equilibrium can be arrived at over a series of sequential steps.

These operations research approaches have been developed mainly by people in business administration, industrial engineering, economics, and mathematics mainly for application to business-oriented problems.[1] In discussing these approaches, however, this paper will use examples generally based on real data involving political policy problems. Doing so requires reasoning by analogy since the goal variables, the activity variables, or both are likely to be noneconomic in nature.

In discussing linear programming, the examples we will use will include the two-activity problem of allocating election campaign funds between mass media expenditures and precinct organization expenditures. Our illustrative multiple-activity problem will consist of optimally allocating civil rights efforts against discrimination in voting, schools, criminal justice, employment, housing, and public accommodations. For a nonlinear problem we return to a two-activity situation involving the attempt to find an optimum mix between law reform activities and routine case handling in the OEO Legal Services Program, where diminishing returns exist between the activities and the goal criterion.

In discussing inventory modeling and the linear optimum level situation we use the policy problem of the optimum level of free press to allow with regard to reporting on matters relevant to a pending criminal trial which might tend to prejudice the defendant's receiving a fair trial. For the nonlinear optimum level situation we use the policy problem of the optimum percentage of defendants to hold in jail pending trial in order to minimize the sum of holding or storage costs (like lost wages), plus our releasing or outage costs (like crime committing while released).

In discussing one-person decision theory, we use the example of a judge deciding whether or not to release a defendant prior to trial, with the key contingent event being whether the defendant will show up in court. One especially important question is how high the probability of the defendant showing up in court has to be before the judge will or should release the defendant. In discussing two-person decision theory and dynamic equilibrium analysis, we use the example of a defendant or defense counsel bargaining with a prosecutor over the sentence the defendant should receive if he pleads guilty with the prosecutor, rather than go to trial. In that situation the defendant is like a buyer haggling to get the price down as low as possible, or at least below his maximum limit, which he has calculated in light of his probable sentence upon going to trial. The prosecutor is thus like a seller haggling to get the price up as high as possible, or at least above his minimum limit, which he has also calculated in light of the probable sentence upon going to trial. Where the two sides are likely to arrive is possibly determinable by a dynamic equilibrium model with the decision theory limits as inputs.

Although this paper attempts to develop operations research methods from the simple to the more complex, it does not presuppose any extensive mathematical knowledge. One welcome aspect of operations research methodology is the fact that there are easy-to-use linear programming routines, regression analysis programs, and other relevant data processing tools readily available at most universities and other computing centers. What arithmetic operations cannot be done with such computer tools can generally be done easily with an electronic calculator, especially those which enable one to quickly raise numbers to unusual exponents as part of the nonlinear aspect of operations research. This paper will not deal with the mathematical theory behind those computer routines, but instead will emphasize how one might organize raw data for an operations research analysis and especially how one might interpret the resulting output.

II. LINEAR PROGRAMMING AND OPTIMUM MIX ANALYSIS

As mentioned in the introduction where linear programming was defined, we will concentrate first on the two-activity linear situation, then the multiple-activity linear situation, and finally the nonlinear situation. One example will be used to illustrate each of these three perspectives, but the same example may also be used in an incidental way to illustrate one or both of the other perspectives. By using three examples, the basic methodological ideas become better reinforced, and the broad applicability of linear programming is also better seen. One cannot, however, so readily discuss a nonlinear example without first presenting it in the simpler linear format. Likewise, one cannot so readily discuss a multiple activity example without first presenting it in the simpler two-activity format.[2]

THE TWO-ACTIVITY SITUATION

The Illustrative Problem

To illustrate on a very simple level what is involved in applying linear programming concepts to a political science problem, let's take the problem of allocating campaign expenditure money to media dollars and precinct organization dollars. Suppose we are working with a Democratic or Republican nonincumbent congressional candidate, who is a member of the minority party in his congressional district running against a nonincumbent, and who wants to allocate his campaign funds between media (that is, TV and radio) dollars and precinct organization (nonmedia) dollars so as to obtain at least 51% of the two-party vote without exceeding his $100,000 campaign budget.[3]

The data for this illustrative example comes from analyzing the votes obtained and the expenditures made by all 58 nonincumbent congressional candidates in 1972 who were members of the previous minority or out-party in their congressional districts running against a nonincumbent. The year 1972 was the first year for which reliable data was available concerning congressional campaign expenditures to supplement other data dealing with TV and radio expenditures and voting tallies.[4]

The same analysis could be done for

(1) incumbents running against nonincumbents,
(2) nonincumbents who are members of the previous majority party running against other nonincumbents, and
(3) nonincumbents running against incumbents.

It makes sense to keep incumbents separate from nonincumbents and in-party candidates separate from out-party candidates because incumbency and membership in the in-party influence the votes one obtains regardless of expenditures, and these factors also influence the dollars one obtains to spend. Incumbents tend to win regardless of how poorly they allocate their substantial funds between media and nonmedia dollars, and nonincumbents running against incumbents tend to lose regardless how well they allocate their generally less substantial funds. The same analysis could also be done for a candidate who has more or less than $100,000 to spend. That, however, is a nice round figure for illustrative purposes, and a realistic one in that about 15% of the 58 out-party nonincumbents running against in-party nonincumbents had more than $100,000 available to spend.

There may be some combination of media and precinct dollars that will enable us to get 51% of the two-party vote while spending substantially less than the $100,000 we have available. Finding that combination is the cost minimization problem. Likewise, there may be some combination of media and precinct dollars that will enable us to get as high a percentage of the two-party vote as possible above 51% while spending no more than the $100,000 we have available. That is the benefit maximization problem. Linear programming is an excellent method for determining what combination of expenditures will minimize costs while achieving at least a minimum benefit level, or determining what combination will maximize benefits while keeping within a maximum cost level.

Linear programming or linear optimizing can be defined as a procedure whereby one finds the optimum allocation of funds or some other scarce resources between two or more alternatives, in light of a given minimizing or maximizing goal, and in light of given constraints or conditions. In order to be linear rather than nonlinear programming, the relations between the resources and the goals must be straight-line or constant-returns relations rather than curved-line or diminishing-returns relations.

For each of the 58 nonincumbent congressional candidates who serve as our data base, we can obtain (%V) the percent of the two-party vote each received in the 1972 election, ($M) the number of TV and radio media dollars each spent for the 1972 election according to the required Federal Communications Commission reports, and ($P) the number of nonmedia dollars each spent according to the required reports of the Office of Federal Elections. Nonmedia dollars are simply the total expenditures minus the TV and radio expenditures. Those nonmedia dollars are mainly used for organizational, canvassing, and precinct activities.

We can then do a regression analysis with media dollars and precinct dollars as the independent variables to predict from, and percent of the two-party vote obtained as the dependent variable to predict to. We are thereby able to induce from the data an empirical equation between those variables of the form $(\%V) = 34\% + .28(\$M) + .17(\$P)$. The 34% in this equation indicates that if no dollars are spent for media or precinct activities, we would predict our candidate would receive about 34% of the two-party vote which of course would make him a loser since he needs 51%. The .28 in this equation indicates that for every extra $1,000 spent on media, approximately one-fourth of an extra percentage point on the two-party vote is obtained. The .17 in this equation indicates that for every extra $1,000 spent on precinct or nonmedia activities, approximately one-sixth of an extra percentage point of the two-party vote is obtained.[5]

In our illustration as in nearly all linear programming situations, the optimum allocation between media dollars and precinct dollars is subject to minimum and maximum constraints. The constraints may be determined by law, by limited finances, by the nature of our measurement, or by other matters. A meaningful way to determine the minimum constraints in this congressional campaign context is to see that the lowest number of TV and radio media dollars needed by those among our 58 candidates who won was $0, and the lowest number of nonmedia dollars needed to win was $26,000. By virtue of the federal Election Campaign Act of 1971, media dollars are limited to $50,000 although the figure is subject to adjustment in light of a cost of living formula and includes newspapers, magazines, outdoor advertising, and certain types of telephone expenses, as well as TV and radio. There is no limit on nonmedia expenditures. Our problem now becomes how to optimally allocate our available budget between $M and $P in light of these additional constraints.

In more general algebraic terms, we can say that linear programming as applied to policy optimizing problems involves either minimizing total costs or maximizing total benefits. Total costs equal the sum of the costs for each policy (that is, $TC = P_1 + P_2$). Total benefits equal the amount of benefits achieved if no effort is expended on any of the policies plus the amount of effort actually expended on each policy weighted by the marginal rate of return, slope, or regression weight of each policy (that is, $TB = a + b_1 P_1 + b_2 P_2$). The right side of either of those two equations can be referred to as the objective function, depending on which is our goal or object, since they are both functions or algebraic equivalents of the variable on the left side.

Likewise, our constraints can be stated algebraically as a series of inequalities of the form $P_1 \geqslant L_1$, $P_2 \geqslant L_2$, $TC \geqslant L_C$, $TB \geqslant L_B$, $P_1 \leqslant H_1$, $P_2 \leqslant H_2$, $TC \leqslant H_C$, and $TB \leqslant H_B$. In these minimum and maximum constraints, L is the lowest limit which is desired, acceptable, or possible, and H is the highest limit which is desired, acceptable, or possible on each variable P_1, P_2, TC, and TB. Linear programming thus involves finding a value for P_1 and P_2 which will satisfy those constraints while minimizing TC, maximizing TB, or optimizing some other objective function as will now be shown graphically and algebraically with the campaign allocation example. Later, problems will be presented in which there are more than two policies (that is, P_1, P_2, ... P_n) and in which the relations between TB and the policies have a nonlinear form like $TB = a(P_1)^{b1}(P_2)^{b2}$.

Graphing the Solution

To better understand what is involved in finding optimum expenditure combinations through linear programming, it is helpful to make a graph depicting the relations among our variables and the constraints on $P, $M, total costs, and total benefits. Figure 1 shows media dollars on the vertical axis and precinct organization dollars on the horizontal axis. It indicates that we cannot spend less than $26,000 on $P and expect to win, and that we cannot spend more than $50,000 on $M and remain within the law.

The figure also shows the maximum cost line connecting (1) the point near the lower right-hand corner of the graph at which $0 is spent for $M and $100 for $P to (2) the point near the upper left-hand corner of the graph where $0 is spent for $P and $100 for $M. Every point on that line involves a combination of $M and $P that adds up to $100 which is why it is also called an equal-cost or constant-cost line.

Figure 1 also shows the minimum benefits line as a straight line connecting two points. The first point near the lower right-hand corner is the point at which $0 is spent for $M, and $100 therefore has to be spent for $P in order for 34% + .17($P) to add up to 51%. The second point midway below the upper left corner is where $0 is spent for $P, and $61 therefore has to be spent for $M in order for 34% + .28($M) to add to 51%. Every point on that line involves a combination of $M and $P that produces 51% of the two-party vote which is why it is also called an equal-benefit line, or a line on which one would be indifferent toward the benefits received from any pair of allocation points.

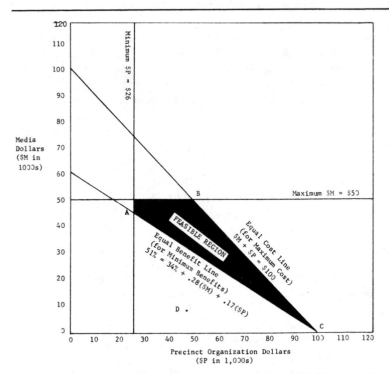

Figure 1: Allocating Media Dollars and Precinct Dollars to Minimize Costs or Maximize Votes (with Constant Returns to Dollars Spent)

Point A is where total cost is minimized, while obtaining at least 51% of the two-party vote.
$M = $45 $P = $26   TC = $71   %V = 51%

Point B is where the vote percentage is maximized, while not spending more than $100.
$M = $50 $P = $50   TC = $100   %V = 57%

Point C is where total cost is maximized and the vote percentage is minimized within the constraints (i.e., the worst allocation within the feasible region).
$M = $0 $P = $100   TC = $100   %V = 51%

Point D represents the average allocation of the 58 non-incumbent out-party 1972 congressional candidates running against non-incumbent in-party candidates.
$M = $9 $P = $47   TC = $56   %V = 45%

Regardless whether we want to minimize costs or maximize benefits, the ideal combination has to be below the maximum cost line. Likewise, it has to be above the minimum benefit line. That ideal or optimum combination also has to be to the right of the minimum $P vertical line and below the maximum $M horizontal line. This means the ideal combination has to be a point somewhere in Figure 1 within the area marked "feasible region" since that is the only area where all four constraints are satisfied simultaneously.

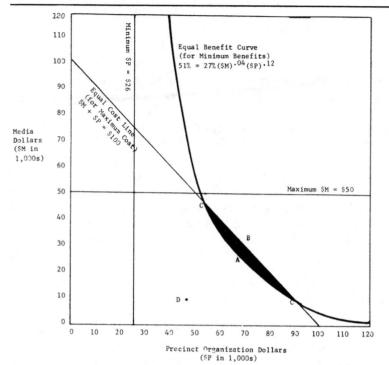

Point A is where total cost is minimized, while obtaining at least 51% of the two-party vote.
       $M = $23 $P = $69   TC = $92   %V = 51%

Point B is where the vote percentage is maximized, while not spending more than $100.
       $M = $30 $P = $70   TC = $100   %V = 52%

Point C is where total cost is maximized and the vote percentage is minimized within
the constraints (i.e., the worst allocation within the feasible region).
       $M = $42 $P = $58   TC = $100   %V = 51%
  or $M = $12 $P = $88   TC = $100   %V = 51%

Point D represents the average allocation of the 58 non-incumbent out-party 1972 congressional candidates running against non-incumbent in-party candidates.
       $M = $9 $P = $47   TC = $55   %V = 45%

**Figure 2: Allocating Media Dollars and Precinct Dollars to Minimize Costs or Maxi-
mize Votes (with Diminishing Returns to Dollars Spent)**

Point A (where $M = $45,000, and $P = $26,000) is the point where
total cost (TC) is minimized while providing about 51% of the two-party
vote. This is because that is the point furthest downward away from the
maximum cost line that is still within the feasible region. By only spending
a total of $71,000, we save $29,000 for between-election expenses, for the
next election, or for other worthwhile causes.

Point B (where $M = $50,000, and $P = $50,000) is the point where
votes are maximized while not spending more than our $100,000. This is

so because that is the point furthest away upward from the minimum benefit line that is still within the feasible region. At that point, 57% of the two-party vote is likely to be obtained since the percent of the two-party vote is predicted to equal 34% + .28($M) + .17($P) by the regression analysis which fits a straight line to the data points for the 58 congressional candidates. One may wish to obtain those extra votes beyond the 51% to insure against miscalculation, to claim a mandate for an aggressive political program, or to satisfy one's ego or other needs.

Note that the minimum benefits line and the minimum $P line represent binding constraints on cost minimization in the sense that we could save additional money if we did not need to satisfy those two constraints. The money we are not saving by virtue of those constraints can be considered an opportunity cost. Likewise note that the maximum total cost line and the maximum $M line both represent binding constraints on benefit maximization in the sense that we could obtain additional votes if we did not need to satisfy those constraints. The extra percentage of the two-party vote we are not obtaining by virtue of those constraints can also be considered an opportunity cost.

An alternative way of interpreting the optimizing of Figure 1 is to use elementary concepts from production and consumption economics. With those concepts, one recognizes that point A is the cost minimization point because there is a family of parallel equal cost lines with one for every possible total cost, and point A is the point where the lowest equal cost line is located, which just barely touches the feasible region. This point can be thought of as the point where the producer of votes minimizes his total costs in allocating his budget to two factors of production—namely media dollars and precinct organization dollars—analogous to labor and capital.

Likewise, point B is the benefit maximization point because there is a family of equal benefit lines with one for every possible %V, and point B is the point where the highest equal benefit line is located which just barely touches the feasible region. This point can be thought of as the point where a consumer purchasing media and precinct organization units maximizes his total utility by optimally allocating his budget between these two consumer goods, analogous to food and clothing.

Variations and Alternatives

It should be noted that one cannot, in our illustration, maximize benefits minus costs. This is so because we do not know how many dollars our candidate considers a given percentage of the two-party vote to be worth. If one percentage point is worth $2,000 in satisfaction to him, then point A maximizes benefits minus costs better than point B since

point A produces $102,000 in benefits at $71,000 in costs for a net benefit of $31,000. Point A, on the other hand, produces $114,000 in benefits
at $100,000 in costs for a net benefit of only $14,000. If, however, one
percentage point is worth $5,000 or more in satisfaction to our candidate,
then point B maximizes benefits minus costs better than point A since
point A produces $204,000 in benefits at $71,000 in costs for a net benefit of $184,000. Point B, on the other hand, then produces $285,000 in
benefits at $100,000 in costs for a higher net benefit of $185,000. In
other words, whether point A or point B is the better point for our candidate depends on whether he considers the extra six percentage points to
be worth the extra $29,000, bearing in mind that he is likely to be a win-
ner under either point A or point B.

Because it may be impossible to convert a nonmonetary benefit like
votes into monetary units, one may have to choose between the goals of
minimizing total costs, maximizing total benefits, or compromising between them. One such compromise might be to optimally allocate our
$100,000 in order to seek 54% of the vote partly because it is the mid-
point between the minimum 51% and the maximum 57% (maximum given
our $100,000 budget) and partly because that seems to be a good insur-
ance figure against miscalculation. In order to determine the optimum
allocation of our budget between $M and $P in this situation, we first
solve for $M in the equation 54% = 34% + .28($M) + .17($26) after setting
$P equal to its minimum since $P has a lower marginal rate of return than
$M. The $M then comes out to be $56 (that is, $56,000) which is higher
than the $50 maximum. We therefore solve for $P in the equation 54% =
34% + .28($50) + .17($P), and $P comes out to be $35. Thus, the optimum allocation between $M and $P to obtain 54% of the vote would be
$50,000 and $35,000 respectively given our linear or constant rate of
return assumption.

An important variation on our basic illustration as depicted in Figure 1
is to substitute a diminishing returns assumption for the linear assumption.
Figure 2 shows the same maximum $M constraint, minimum $P constraint,
and maximum TC constraint as in Figure 1. The equal benefit line, however, this time is shown as a curve. The equation for that curve was determined by doing a regression analysis with the logarithms of the %V, $M,
and $P for each of the 58 candidates, rather than just using the original
values of %V, $M, and $P. Working with those logarithms in effect takes
into consideration the fact that additional dollars spent for either $M or
$P produce additional votes, but at a decreasing or diminishing rate.[6]

More specifically, the logarithmic approach generates an equation of
the form $\%V = 27\%(\$M)^{.04}(\$P)^{.12}$. This equation indicates that under
the nonlinear or diminishing returns assumption, we would predict a non-

incumbent out-party candidate would get about 27% of the two-party vote by just spending $1 (that is, $1,000) for $M and $1 for $P. The equation also shows that by increasing $M by 100%, the vote percentage will go up 4%. Likewise, by increasing $P by 100%, the vote percentage will go up 12%, which means that under the nonlinear assumption, $P has a higher marginal rate of return than $M. The feasible region into which the optimum allocation must occur is the shaded area of the figure where all the constraints are simultaneously satisfied. Point A is the cost minimization point where $M equals $23, $P equals $69, and 51% of the vote is predicted to be obtained. Point B is the benefit maximization point where $M equals $30, $P equals $70, and the percent of the two-party vote is only slightly higher (52%), given the increasingly greater difficulty of obtaining additional votes. An exact method for determining those calculations is discussed later, using the allocations of the OEO Legal Services Program to law reform and case handling as an example, but one can readily see the approximate allocation in Figure 2 once the lines and the curve have been drawn.[7]

An alternative way of expressing the same ideas shown in either Figure 1 or Figure 2 is to plot a series of graphs in which a goal variable is shown on the vertical axis (either minimizing TC or maximizing %V), and a policy variable is shown on the horizontal axis (either $M or $P). This would result in four such graphs for the linear assumption and four for the nonlinear assumption. For example, to show the relation between %V and $M two-dimensionally while considering all the constraints means plotting the equation %V = 34% + .28($M) + .17($100-$M), where $100-$M substitutes for $P and shows that we want to spend our whole $100 to maximize %V. Similar equations can be developed relating each goal variable to each policy variable while simultaneously considering whatever is necessary on the other variables and the constraints. Some people find this alternative perspective to be easier to grasp or to provide supplementary insights although it involves more equations and more graphs.

Another variation on the basic scheme is to recognize that there can be more than two categories of activities with regard to election campaign expenditures. We might for instance want to arrive at an optimum allocation among dollars spent for

(1) media advertising for the election campaign,
(2) precinct canvassing also for the election campaign, and
(3) precampaign registration activities.

As an alternative example, we might be concerned with subdividing media dollars into radio, television, newspapers, billboards, and other media.

How to handle those kinds of multiple-activity situations will be discussed in the next section, using the civil rights allocation problem as an illustrative example.[8]

THE MULTIPLE-ACTIVITY SITUATION

The Basic Data

In 1969, questionnaires were mailed by the Chicago office of the NAACP to an undetermined set of NAACP chapter presidents. The mailing generated 32 completed questionnaires from 32 cities across the country. The questions were designed mainly to determine 12 items of information, although doing so involved averaging numerous items on the questionnaire. Six of the 12 composite items relate to efforts or inputs exerted in each city for the five-year period prior to 1969 with regard to reducing discrimination or improving equality in voting (V), schools (S), criminal justice (C), employment (E), housing (H), and public accommodations (A). The other six items relate to benefits or outputs obtained in each city for the five-year period prior to 1969 with regard to the same civil rights fields. Both the input and the output variables are measured on a five-point scale of big increase, small increase, no change, small decrease, and big decrease. For each city, the six output variables are averaged in order to create an overall goal variable of equality improvement (EQ). The six input variables are sometimes divided into two groups covering efforts against mainly governmental discrimination (voting, schools, and criminal justice) and efforts against mainly private discrimination (employment, housing, and public accommodations), with a separate average score for each of those two general input variables given to each city. The main purpose of the analysis is to obtain some insights into what is involved in allocating scarce resources among the various civil rights activities in order to maximize equality improvement.[9]

Figure 3 provides a graphic analysis of the problem of choosing between two activity groupings. The vertical axis shows effort against governmental discrimination (G), and the horizontal axis shows effort against private discrimination (P), as the two activities between which we are seeking an optimum mix. Both activities are measured on the five-point scale previously mentioned. The horizontal line extending eastward from the 5-level on the G scale, and the vertical line extending northward from the 5-level on the P scale indicate that the scales only go as high as a big increase. The horizontal line extending eastward from the 3-level on the G scale and the vertical line extending northward from the 3-level on the P scale indicate that the civil rights decision-makers would probably not

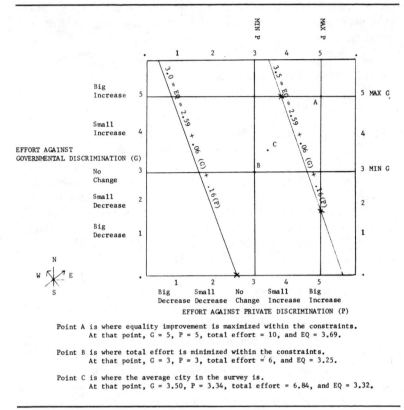

Point A is where equality improvement is maximized within the constraints. At that point, G = 5, P = 5, total effort = 10, and EQ = 3.69.

Point B is where total effort is minimized within the constraints. At that point, G = 3, P = 3, total effort = 6, and EQ = 3.25.

Point C is where the average city in the survey is. At that point, G = 3.50, P = 3.34, total effort = 6.84, and EQ = 3.32.

Figure 3: Allocating Effort Against Governmental Discrimination and Private Discrimination to Maximize Equality Improvement

want a decrease in effort against discrimination in either of the civil rights activity groupings although one could work with other minimum constraints.

The two diagonal lines are equal-benefit lines. Any allocation to G and P along the first line provides an equality improvement score of 3.0 or no change, which is probably the minimum that the civil rights decision-makers would like to have. Any allocation to G and P along the second line which is further toward the northeast provides an equality improvement score of 3.5, or a change between no change and a small increase. The coefficients of 2.59, .06, and .16 for both of those lines were determined by inputting into a computer the EQ, G, and P score for each of the 32 cities along with a linear regression analysis program. Once those coefficients are determined, the first line can be plotted by

(1) setting EQ equal to 3.0, G equal to 0, and solving for P to determine one point;

(2) setting EQ equal to 3.0, P equal to 0, and solving for G to determine a second point; and then

(3) connecting those two points.

One can do likewise with the 3.5 line although G and P can be set to numbers other than 0 if the 0 level is too far off the graph.

The region that is simultaneously within the horizontal constraints on G, the vertical constraints on P, and the diagonal constraints on EQ at 3.0 and 5.0 constitutes a feasible region in the sense that any point in that region produces a satisfactory although not necessarily an optimizing solution. There are two optimizing points in Figure 4 within the feasible region. Point B is the allocation point where one maximizes the goal variable while not exceeding the total effort available. The total effort available is 5 units on G and 5 units on P. That also happens to be the optimum allocation if one wants to maximize equality improvement. At that allocation, one obtains an equality improvement score of 3.69 which is the maximum possible within the feasible region. The presence of other variables which are influential in changing EQ (like increased societal affluence and education) is partly indicated by the fact that expending all our civil rights inputs only produces an EQ of 3.69, and by the fact that G and P collectively only account for about one-fifth of the variance on EQ. Point A is the allocation point where one minimizes total effort while providing at least a minimum level on the goal variable. Point A (which involves an allocation of 3 units to G and 3 units to P) yields an EQ level of 3.25 which is above the minimum 3.0 level and still within the constraints. This means that even if there is no change on G and no change on P, EQ will still go up slightly because of demographic or other variables which are influential in changing EQ. What we have done is analogous to what the rational consumer is supposed to do when he or she decides on an optimum mix between competing goods where the benefits are not measured in the same units as the costs.

The Multiple-Activity Graph

If we want to know what the optimum mix is among the six civil rights activities rather than the two groups of civil rights activities, we can feed into a computer a value for each of the cities for EQ, V, S, C, E, H, and A, along with a linear regression analysis program. Doing so generates the regression equation EQ = 2.54 + .04(V) + .32(S) + .01(C) − .02(E) − .04(H) − .08(A). The reason some variables have a negative regression coefficient is that those coefficients indicate the relation between each activity and EQ when the other five activities are held constant. An activity will tend to have a negative regression coefficient if it has relatively low although positive correlation with EQ (compared to the other variables which are held constant) and a relatively high positive correlation with those other variables.[10]

This equation cannot be shown in a two-dimensional graph like Figure 3 which was used to plot the two-dimensional equation $EQ = 2.59 + .06(G) + .16(P)$ at various category levels of equality improvement like 3.0 and 3.5. In that graph, one axis consisted of effort against governmental discrimination, and the other axis consisted of effort against private discrimination. It is impossible to draw a graph with six axes all of which are perpendicular to each other in order to plot a six-dimensional equality improvement contour or hyperplane at a level of 3.0, 3.5, or any other level. One can, however, draw a two-dimensional graph with equality improvement on the vertical axis and the effort categories on the horizontal axis as is done in Figure 4. Both Figures 3 and 4 are unnecessary to doing the linear programming, but they provide useful visual aids.

The horizontal line extending rightward from the 5-level on equality improvement shows that the scale does not allow for equality improvement greater than a big increase, which is scored 5.0. The vertical line extending upward from the 5-level on effort against discrimination likewise shows that the effort scale does not allow for an effort greater than a big increase on any of the six effort dimensions. The horizontal line extending rightward from the 3-level on equality improvement indicates that the civil rights decision-makers are not likely to approve any combination of effort expenditures that will result in less than no change. In other words, they are not likely to approve a combination that will result in a decrease in equality improvement or at least a decrease in equality. Unfortunately, the questionnaire did not ask the respondents questions about absolute equality, only about equality improvement. It is possible that the decision-makers would be satisfied with a decrease in marginal equality improvement or a decrease in the incremental improvement in equality if absolute equality were already quite high. Nevertheless, the same kind of methodological analysis that is applied here with equality improvement categories could be applied with absolute equality categories. Likewise, the vertical line extending upward from the 3-level on effort against discrimination is there on the assumption that the civil rights decision-makers would not want a decrease in effort against discrimination in any of the six civil rights fields. One could draw other minimum levels on equality improvement and effort against discrimination (such as the 1.00 level on both), and then arrive at other optimum allocations of effort

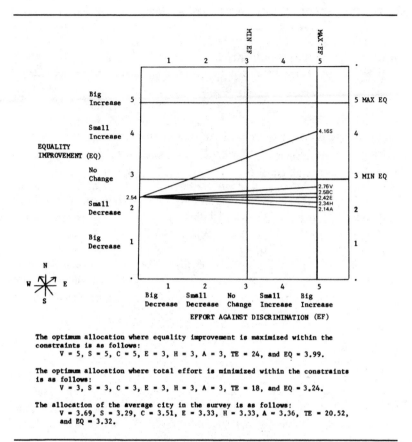

The optimum allocation where equality improvement is maximized within the constraints is as follows:
  V = 5, S = 5, C = 5, E = 3, H = 3, A = 3, TE = 24, and EQ = 3.99.

The optimum allocation where total effort is minimized within the constraints is as follows:
  V = 3, S = 3, C = 3, E = 3, H = 3, A = 3, TE = 18, and EQ = 3.24.

The allocation of the average city in the survey is as follows:
  V = 3.69, S = 3.29, C = 3.51, E = 3.33, H = 3.33, A = 3.36, TE = 20.52, and EQ = 3.32.

Figure 4: Allocating Effort Among Six Civil Rights Activities to Maximize Equality Improvement

among the civil rights activities using the same reasoning and methodology as is applied here.[11]

Each of the six sloping lines in Figure 4 corresponds to one of the six civil rights activities. All the sloping lines begin at 2.54 on the equality improvement vertical axis because the regression analysis indicates that there would be equality improvement at the 2.54 level even if no effort were exerted on each of the six dimensions, given the occurrence of other variables which produce equality improvement. A 2.54 equality improvement means a decrease between no change and a small decrease.

Some of the lines in Figure 4 slope upward (such as the lines for schools, voting, and criminal justice), whereas some of the lines slope downward (employment, housing, and public accommodations). Whether the lines slope upward or downward depends on whether the regression weights or slopes in the six-dimensional regression equation are positive or negative. A regression weight can be negative if the civil rights activity with which it is associated increases while equality improvement decreases because of adverse changes which simultaneously occur in other civil rights activities.

The degree of slope for any of the six activities reflects the size of the regression weight. In effect, each line shows the relation between each civil rights activity and its equality improvement if the other five activities are scored zero on the effort scale. For example, the V line starts at 2.54 when V = 0 and rises to 2.74 when V = 5 since 2.74 = 2.54 + .04(5) when S, C, E, H, and A all equal 0. It is not so easy to conceptualize verbally a zero point on the effort scale since a score of one was the lowest score provided for on the questionnaire, although the questionnaire items could have been scored 0, 1, 2, 3, and 4 rather than 1, 2, 3, 4, and 5. It is, however, easy to conceptualize visually a zero point on Figure 4 since it is the same distance below the one point as the one is below the two. Since the zero point can be visualized easily on the graph but not verbalized, it is the opposite of the conceptualization problem involved in the notion of six-dimensionality which can be verbalized easily, but cannot be visualized with six perpendicular axes.

Finding the Optimum Allocations

Given the information contained in Figure 4, it is easy to determine the optimum allocation among the six civil rights activities if one is seeking to maximize the amount of equality improvement without exceeding an effort score of 5.0 on each activity (that is, goal B). Given that goal, those constraints, and the relation between equality improvement and the six activities, one would logically want to have the minimum effort possible exerted toward employment, housing, and public accommodations (that is, an effort at the 3.0 level) in view of their negative regression slopes. Likewise, one would logically want to have the maximum effort possible exerted toward schools, voting, and criminal justice (that is, an effort at the 5.0 level) in view of their positive regression slopes, provided that a maximum effort on these three activities does not cause equality improvement to exceed wastefully its 5.0 maximum. If in the multiple regression equation, the value of E, H, and A is set at the minimum of 3.0 and the value of V, S, and C is set at the maximum of 5.0, then when one solves for EQ in the equation, one gets a value of 3.99 or EQ* (which is the EQ when resources are optimally allocated to V, S, C, E, H, and A to maximize EQ subject to the constraints). This is the highest amount of equality improvement one can obtain by allocating no less than three and no more than five units of effort to each of the civil rights activities. This amount of equality improvement, however, is less than the 5.0 maximum equality improvement, and therefore one need not bring down C, V, or S from 5.0 to get equality improvement down below 5.0.

If the maximizing allocation did produce equality improvement greater than 5.0 through an unreasonable amount of effort on each activity, then one would first bring down C since it has the lowest and thus least efficient upward slope. Efficiency is the ratio between effort and results or between change in effort and change in results. If bringing C down to 3.0 does not bring EQ down to 5.0, then one would logically next bring V down and finally S. Linear programming routines which are available at most major university computing centers can be used to determine exactly how much to bring down C, V, or S under those circumstances.

Given the information contained in Figure 4, it is likewise easy to determine the optimum allocation among the six civil rights activities if one is seeking to minimize the total effort without falling below an equality improvement score of 3.0 (that is, goal A). Such a cost minimization allocation, rather than one emphasizing benefit maximization, might involve allocating the minimum 3.0 effort to each of the six civil rights activities (for an optimum or minimum total effort of 18 units or EF*), provided that such an across-the-board effort minimization does not produce less than a 3.0 equality improvement. Substituting 3's for V, S, C, E, H, and A in the multiple-activity regression equation yields an equality improvement score of 3.24. Such a score does satisfy the minimum equality improvement constraint.

If, however, allocating 3's to all the civil rights activities does not produce an equality improvement score of at least 3.0, then one should logically move the schools effort up from 3.0 toward 5.0, and then check to see if EQ comes up to its minimum. If that does not work, then try moving up to V and C in that order. That is the logical order since effort expended on school discrimination is the most productive, useful, or efficient of the six activities. To raise EQ, one would not want to move E, H, or A up from 3.0 since doing so would lower EQ given the negative regression weights of those activities with EQ. In other words, if a linear programming approach does not get EQ up to 3.0 when S, V, and C are at 5.0 and E, H, and A are at 3.0, then there is no feasible allocation that will satisfy the minimum equality improvement constraint. Under those circumstances, one would have to

(1) accept the best equality improvement available even though it is below 3.0,

(2) lower the 3.0 minimum EQ constraint,

(3) find a way of increasing the productivity or efficiency of one or more of the six civil rights activities,

(4) revise the measurement system so as to allow the more efficient activities like schools and voting to be able to meaningfully absorb an expenditure of effort greater than 5.0, or

(5) lower the constraints on the activities with the negative coefficients.

At first glance, the optimum equality improvement of 3.99 through the benefit maximization approach may not seem much greater than the empirical equality improvement of 3.32 which the average city in the sample had. If one thinks in percentage terms, however, then 3.99 is 120% of 3.32. It might also be noted that the cost minimization approach satisfies the 3.0 equality improvement constraint with a total effort of 18, which is 88% of the 20.52 empirical total effort expended by the average city. These comparisons between the optimum allocations and the empirical allocation further bring out the value of a linear programming perspective in more efficiently allocating scarce resources in order to maximize benefits without exceeding one's budget, or to minimize costs without falling below one's prescribed minimum benefit level.

Variations on the Basic Model

Another variation on the basic model (besides the multiple-activity variation) is to fit a nonlinear regression line to the data in order to reflect the phenomenon of diminishing returns which may be present. To do so for the two-activity example, we can feed into a computer a value for each of the cities for the logarithms of EQ, G, and P. Doing so generates the regression equation $EQ = 2.29(G)^{-.05}(P)^{.35}$. However, this more complicated regression equation with its decimal exponents did not fit our range of empirical data substantially better than our linear regression equation. To find the optimum mix points with such a nonlinear regression equation requires a kind of nonlinear marginal analysis like that discussed in the next section, with regard to finding an optimum point on a nonlinear total benefit curve.

Another important variation is to allow the constraints to vary. A binding constraint is one that is keeping us from maximizing total benefits or minimizing total costs; we can see how much of a missed opportunity that binding constraint is causing us. This raises the concept of opportunity costs which refer to the equality improvement (or saving of total effort) which one is missing by operating under constraints that limit the available allocations. In the benefit maximization allocation, one could obtain more equality improvement if it were possible to raise S, V, and C above 5.0 or if it were possible to lower E, H, and A below 3.0. To determine the exact amount of equality improvement one is missing, one can raise S, V, or C one unit or lower E, H, or A one unit and then recalculate EQ. Likewise, in the cost minimization allocation, one could save more total effort and still not go below a 3.0 equality improvement if it were possible to lower S, V, C, E, H, and A below 3.0. To determine the amount of total effort that could be saved, one should set EQ at 3.0 and have the linear programming routine calculate the values of V, S, C, E, H, and A which will minimize TE while still providing an EQ of 3.0. If effort expended on the civil rights activities can go as low as a score of 1.0 rather than 3.0 (and as high as a score of 5.0), then the allocation which minimizes total effort and provides an EQ of 3.0 will be an allocation of 1.0 to every activity except schools and an allocation of 1.7 to schools. Total effort is then at a minimum of 6.7 effort units.

Possibly the most interesting variations are those that involve varying the input levels (X) to see the effect on one or more output levels (Y), while holding constant the regression coefficients (b); or varying the desired output levels (Y) to see what input changes (X) might be necessary to achieve those new output levels, while holding constant the regression coefficients (b). Closely related although generally not quite as interesting are scenarios which involve

(1) varying b to see the effect on Y while holding X constant,
(2) varying b to see what new X would be needed if Y were held constant,
(3) varying X to see how b must have changed if Y is held constant, and
(4) varying Y to see how b must have changed if X is held constant.

In order to make the model fit the data better and to provide further insights into the causal implications of the model, it is helpful to divide the sample of cities into northern cities and southern cities or to add a dichotomous region variable to the two-activity variables. By creating a regression equation for each subsample, we are thereby able to account for substantially more of the variance on the EQ dependent variable with each of the regression equations than we could with the single regression equation shown in Figure 4. Region was not, however, found to be an intervening variable causing both high inputs and high outputs in the south so as to make the input-output correlations spurious. Instead the inputs were lower in the south (possibly due to less black militancy and more white resistance), and the outputs were higher in the south (possibly due to starting from a lower equality base on which it is easier to improve).

Including other demographic variables in the model such as city size, city wealth, or percent black population might also improve its predictive power and its ability to generate causal insights. The stronger the causal predictive power of the model and the more meaningful the sample and measurement, the more useful the model is for making policy recommendations with regard to the optimum mix of effort activities or other scarce resources.

THE NONLINEAR SITUATION

The Basic Data

A substantial literature has developed concerning how the OEO Legal Services Program should allocate its resources between routine case handling and broader law reform activities. Unfortunately, most of the literature tends to be somewhat emotional and lacking in quantitative data. One purpose of this section is to analyze some of the vast amount of evaluation data which has been gathered by the Auerbach management consulting firm in order to see what light it sheds on this much debated issue.[12]

Figure 5 summarizes the portions of the Auerbach data which are especially relevant to the law reform versus case handling issue. It shows that the average legal services agency (for which data was available) had a 1970 budget of $68.34 per participant (that is, $68.34 was the average budget). Figure 5 also shows (point D) that the average agency spent $62.18 (or 91% of that money) on case handling and $6.16 (or 9%) on law reform and related activities. These reform activities included changing laws or administrative practices, economic development, community education, and group representation. A key issue is how much of that $68.34 should be spent for law reform, and how much for case handling in light of the Auerbach evaluation of the agencies.

Figure 5 considers the ideal allocation to law reform to be between a minimum of 10% of the budget and a maximum of 20%, which means case handling should be between 80% and 90%. These figures were arrived at by analyzing the verbal categories which the Auerbach evaluation teams used in making their evaluations, and by analyzing the actual distribution of allocations among the approximately 250 agencies involved. The methodology of the optimizing analysis for which Figure 5 can be used, however, is the same regardless what maximums and minimums we use with regard to law reform and case handling.

A key constraint is the maximum total cost line for the average agency which was arrived at by determining

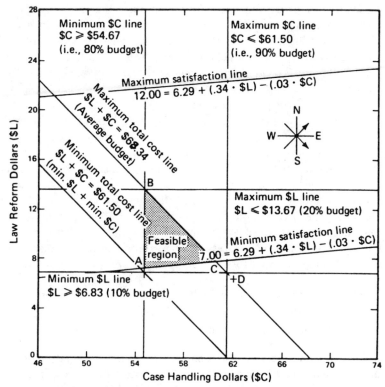

Point A is where total cost is minimized within the constraints.
$$\$L = \$7.06 \qquad \$C = \$54.67 \qquad \%C = \$61.74 \qquad S = 7.00$$

Point B is where satisfaction is maximized within the constraints.
$$\$L = \$13.67 \qquad \$C = \$54.67 \qquad TC = \$68.34 \qquad S = 9.27$$

Point C is where total cost is maximized and satisfaction is minimized within the constraints.
$$\$L = \$7.46 \qquad \$C = \$60.88 \qquad TC = \$68.34 \qquad S = 7.00$$

Point D is where the average LSP agency in the survey is.
$$\$L = \$6.16 \qquad \$C = \$62.18 \qquad TC = \$68.34 \qquad S = 6.51$$

All dollar amounts refer to dollars per planned participant.

Figure 5: Allocating Dollars to Law Reform and Case Handling to Minimize Costs or Maximize Benefits (with Constant Returns and a Positively-Sloped Equal-Benefit Line)

(1) the total budget for each agency and dividing by the number of its planned participants,

(2) summing these budget-over-participants figures for all the agencies, and then

(3) dividing by the number of agencies.

This is a key constraint because it determines how far we can go in spending money per participant to maximize the satisfaction of the evaluators without exceeding our budget. The maximum cost line is an equal-cost line such that the number of law reform dollars plus the number of case handling dollars spent at any point on the line will add up to $68.34.

The other key constraint is the minimum total satisfaction level. This is a key constraint because it determines how far we can go in *not* spending money per participant if we want to minimize our total costs without falling below a minimum satisfaction level at evaluation time. The minimum satisfaction line is an equal-satisfaction line such that the number of law reform dollars plus the number of case handling dollars spent at any point on the line will add up to 7.00 units of satisfaction. In the evaluation questionnaire which the evaluators used, being above 7.00 units of satisfaction meant "project operating efficiently"; whereas being below 7.00 meant "project has internal problems." To determine the formula to find what combinations of law reform and case handling dollars yield 7.00 units of satisfaction, it is necessary to perform a regression analysis in which the computer input for each agency consists of

(1) its evaluation satisfaction score,

(2) its expenditure for law reform, and

(3) its expenditure for case handling.

The minimum total cost line is an equal-cost line pegged at $61.50 because the minimum $L that should be spent is $6.83 (or 10% of the budget as mentioned above), and the minimum $C that should be spent is $64.67 (or 80% of the budget). The maximum satisfaction line is an equal satisfaction line pegged at 12.00 units because that is as high as the evaluation scale provided for. Given all these lines, the only feasible allocation of the budget between law reform and case handling is an allocation point somewhere in the black triangle area of Figure 5, designated the feasible region. But where?

Some Linear Solutions

Point A (where $L equals $7.07, and $C = $54.67) is the point where total cost is minimized while providing at least 7.00 satisfaction units. This is so because it is the point furthest away from the maximum cost line but still within the feasible region. By spending only $61.74, we save $6.60 or about 10% per participant and still meet our minimum 7.00 satisfaction level. In reality, the average amount spent per participant was $68.34, and yet because the $68.34 was not optimally allocated, the average legal services agency in the Auerbach data had a satisfaction score of only 6.45 units. On an annual budget of 60 to 70 million dollars, 10% saved would provide a lot of funds for opening new legal services agencies or expanding old ones.

Point B (where $L = \$13.67$, and $C = \$54.67$) is the point where total satisfaction is maximized while not spending more than $68.34 per participant. This is so because it is the point furthest away from the minimum benefit line but is still within the feasible region. By spending our $68.34 in this manner, we can achieve 9.27 units of satisfaction rather than the 6.45 units which the average legal services agency actually received by the Auerbach evaluators. An increase from 6.45 to 9.27 is a 44% gain. To have the legal services program or any governmental program produce 44% more satisfaction without spending additional money, by merely reallocating its expenditures, seems to be a change worth adopting, or at least worth looking into.

Note that if one were interested in minimizing costs while maintaining a 7.00 minimum satisfaction level, one might be able to save even more money by spending less than 80% of the budget on case handling, assuming the same relations hold outside the constraint lines. With those relations as given, if there were no minimum case handling constraint, then by spending nothing on case handling and spending $2.09 on law reform, we can still obtain 7.00 satisfaction units. Note also that if one were interested in maximizing satisfaction without exceeding the $68.34 average expenditure per participant, then perhaps one could obtain even more satisfaction by spending more than 20% of the budget on law reform. With the relations as given, if there were no maximum law reform constraint, by spending 100% of a smaller budget on law reform or $16.80, we can achieve the 12.00 maximum satisfaction level.

These findings tend to show that money can be saved and satisfaction increased by a greater allocation to law reform and a lesser allocation to case handling either within the 80%-20% and 90%-10% constraints or within another set of constraints which allows for more law reform and less case handling. The fact that these are the findings reflects the reaction of the evaluators to law reform and case handling activities. Another set of evaluators would probably have arrived at a different set of evaluations (that is, a different set of satisfaction scores for the legal services agencies), although the new set might also reveal the need for more law reform and less case handling. The original evaluators consisted of teams of practicing lawyers, law professors, former legal services attorneys, and community analysts whom the Auerbach Corporation, in conjunction with the Office of Legal Services and the National Legal Aid and Defender Association, considered to be experts in evaluating legal service agencies.

As a compromise between minimizing costs and maximizing goals, we could choose a $L of $10.37 which is the midpoint between $7.07 (the cost minimization position) and $13.67 (the benefit maximization position). Doing so will mean a compromise $C of $54.67, TC of $65.04, and S of 8.18. If one accepts this optimum position, it means recommending an expenditure of 80% of each agency's budget to case handling and $10.37/$68.34 or 18% to law reform. A similar percentage breakdown could be applied to the total national budget available for legal services programs.

Many other things can be done and are being done with the Auerbach data. Particularly interesting is work being done on determining what agency characteristics bear a correlation or causal relation with high satisfaction scores, including the characteristics of the agency personnel, the local bar, the poverty community, and the geographical region, as well as expenditures for law reform and case handling. Thus far it appears that the amount spent for law reform within the constraints given is the most important determinant of satisfactory agency operation. This finding is something many legal services attorneys have said is so without doing a quantitative analysis although critics of the law reform approach have just as strongly argued the opposite viewpoint.

Cost Minimization with Diminishing Returns

Although Figure 5 complies with the Auerbach empirical data, it is unusual to have benefit lines that are positively sloped from southeast to northwest rather than inversely sloped from northeast to southwest. In other words, it is more common for Activity 1 dollars and Activity 2 dollars to move in opposite directions in order to hold total benefits constant than to move in the same direction. A positively or negatively sloped equal benefit line has no effect on the procedures used in linear programming where all the relations are straight lines. Such a line, however, does affect the appropriate methodology for optimizing costs or benefits when diminishing returns are involved.[13]

In order to demonstrate how one minimizes costs and maximizes benefits with a diminishing returns equal benefit line that is negatively sloped, as is more commonly the case, let us assume the relation between S, $L, and $C is $S = .7 \cdot \sqrt[3]{\$L} \cdot \sqrt{\$C} = .7 \cdot \$L^{.33} \cdot \$C^{.33}$. By changing the plus and minus signs to multiplication signs, the relation between $C and S is changed from negative to positive, and the relation between $C and $L is changed from positive to negative. By changing the regression coefficients from multipliers to exponents, the relation between inputs of $C and $L and the output of S becomes a nonlinear diminishing returns relation. This

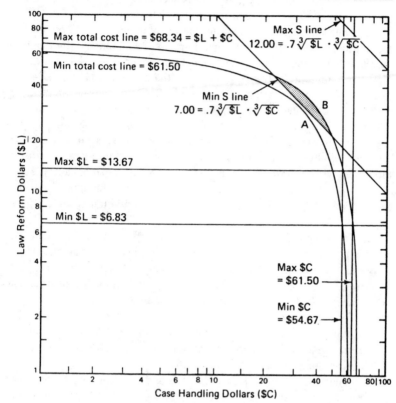

Point A is where total cost is minimized while providing at least 7.00 units of satisfaction.
    $L = \$31.62   \$C = \$31.62   TC = \$63.24   S = 7.00$

Point B is where satisfaction is maximized while not spending more than $68.34.
    $L = \$34.17   \$C = \$34.17   TC = \$68.34   S = 7.37$

Figure 6: Allocating Dollars to Law Reform and Case Handling to Minimize Costs or Maximize Benefits (with Diminishing Returns and a Negatively-Sloped Equal-Benefit Line)

is so in the sense that as we add more $C or $L, we get more S, but at a diminishing rate. Figure 6 shows on logarithmic interval axes the minimum and maximum satisfaction lines corresponding to this new equal benefit equation.[14] Logarithmic paper is used because it converts the equal benefit curve into a straight line which makes it easier to plot, although the simpler equal-cost line then comes out curved.

To illustrate how to minimize costs at a minimum level of satisfaction or maximize satisfaction at a maximum level of costs using the total cost and total benefit lines of Figure 6, it is necessary to ignore the minimum and maximum $L and $C constraint lines. This is so because if those lines are complied with, there is no point on the minimum satisfaction line that is simultaneously between the minimum and maximum $L lines and the minimum and maximum $C lines. Let us make the reasonable assumption that the minimum $L is zero dollars and the maximum $L is $68.34, and that likewise the minimum $C is zero dollars and the maximum $C is $68.34. In other words, let us remove the minimum and maximum constraints on the separate activity variables as is often done in linear programming problems and see what happens. One obvious happening is that the new feasible region is the shaded area between the minimum satisfaction line and the maximum total cost line. What is not so obvious is exactly what point within that shaded area is the optimum minimum cost point for allocating $L and $C, and what point is the optimum maximum benefit point.

The cost minimization point is at point A. Geometrically, this corresponds to a point on the minimum satisfaction line that is about midway between the two points where the minimum satisfaction line intersects the maximum total cost line. That is the point within the new feasible region that is furthest away from the maximum total cost line and closest to the former minimum total cost line. Actually, there is no longer a minimum total cost line if there is no longer a minimum $L or minimum $C. Therefore, what was formerly the minimum total cost line should be referred to as an equal cost line equal to $61.50.

To determine exactly where point A is and the value of $L and $C at that point, one must first state $L in terms of $C in the revised version of the minimum satisfaction formula which is $7.00 = .7 \cdot \sqrt[3]{\$L} \cdot \sqrt[3]{\$C}$. This means $\$L = [7.00/(.7 \cdot \sqrt[3]{\$C})]^3$ which simplifies to $\$L = 1000/\$C$. If we know that total cost = $L + $C, then we also know that total cost = $(1000/\$C) + \$C$. We have thus stated TC in terms of just $C, after having stated $L in terms of $C at the minimum S level desired.

We must next find the calculus derivative or slope of the total cost with respect to $C for the equation, total cost = $(1000/\$C) + \$C$. The derivative of Y (a dependent variable) with respect to X (an independent variable) is the number corresponding to the ratio between a change in Y and a change in X when the value of the change in X becomes so small as to approach zero, but not quite reach it. A derivative can also be thought of as the algebraic expression for the slope of the tangent to a curve at any given point on the curve such as the point where the curve is at a minimum or maximum. Fortunately, tables are available whereby one can read off the derivative of any expression without fully understanding what a derivative is.[15] Such a table indicates that the derivative of the total cost with respect to $C is $(-1000/\$C^2) + 1$. In other words, where TC = $(1000/\$C) + \$C$, or TC = $1000 \cdot \$C^{-1} + \$C$, then the ratio or slope between a change in TC and a change in $C equals $(-1000/\$C^2) + 1$.

We can then set this derivative equal to zero which means we are now at a point where there is no slope or a horizontal slope between total costs and $C, and total costs are thus at a minimum at the 7.00 given level of satisfaction. We then solve for $C at this point. If $(-1000/\$C^2) + 1 = 0$, then C = $31.62. For the final step, we plug this value of $C into the equation 7.00 = $.7 \cdot \sqrt[3]{\$L} \cdot \sqrt[3]{\$C}$, and then solve for $L. Doing so reveals that the optimum $L is also $31.62. Thus, at point A, the total cost is $63.24 with a satisfaction level of 7.00.

What we have in effect done through the above use of differential calculus is to find the value of $L and $C at the point where the lowest possible total cost line just barely touches the minimum satisfaction line. This lowest total cost line has a value of $63.24 at any point along the line. A total cost line one penny less than $63.24 (if the arithmetic is done accurately) would not quite touch up to or be tangent to the minimum S line, and thus would insufficiently produce less than 7.00 satisfaction units. Likewise, a total cost line one penny more than $63.24 would intersect the minimum S line rather than just barely touch it, and would excessively produce more than 7.00 satisfaction units.

Note that the optimum solution involved spending some money for law reform and some money for case handling even though there was no minimum $L and no minimum $C, and thus in terms of the constraints, all of the money could have been spent for $L. The reason some money was spent for $L and some for $C is because in setting up the hypothetical relation between S, $L, and $C which would show a negatively sloping equal benefit line, we gave $L and $C equal weight in determining S since the cube root is taken of both $L and $C in the formula. This not only causes some $L and some $C to be spent in the optimum solution, but also causes equal amounts to be spent on $L and $C. However, even if the weight given to $L had been substantially greater (such as by only taking the square root of $L in the nonlinear equation), some money would still probably be spent on $C in the optimum solution. This is so because although at lower expenditure levels it would be more efficient to spend on $L, the phenomenon of diminishing returns would cause continued spending on $L to become inefficient relative to spending on $C. This point of inefficiency might be reached before enough money could be spent on $L to produce a 7.00 minimum satisfaction level.

The only binding constraint in this cost minimization situation is the minimum satisfaction line. If it were lowered, additional savings could be had and opportunity costs avoided. As before, however, we cannot judge whether lowering the minimum S line would be worth the dollars saved without knowing how many dollars one satisfaction unit is worth. With a minimum S line of 7.00, there is a savings of $5.10 from the $68.34 available per participant. This savings, however, is as hypothetical as the slope and shape of the minimum benefit line.

Benefit Maximization with Diminishing Returns

The benefit maximization point is at point B. Geometrically, this corresponds to a spoint on the maximum total cost line that is about midway between the two points where the minimum satisfaction line intersects the maximum total cost line. That is the point within the feasible region that is furthest away from the minimum S line of 7.00 and closest to the maximum S line of 12.00.

To determine exactly where point B is and the value of $L and $C at that point, one must first state $L in terms of $C in the maximum budget formula which is $68.34 = $L + $C. This mean $L = $68.34 − $C. If we know that satisfaction units obtained = $.7 \cdot \sqrt[3]{\$L} \cdot \sqrt[3]{\$C}$, then we also know that satisfaction = $.7 \cdot \sqrt[3]{\$68.34 - \$C} \cdot \sqrt[3]{\$C}$. We have thus stated S in terms of $C, after having stated $L in terms of $C at the maximum TC level available. We must next find the calculus derivative of satisfaction (as the dependent variable) with respect to $C (as the independent variable) for the equation $S = .7 \cdot \sqrt[3]{\$68.34 - \$C} \cdot \sqrt[3]{\$C}$. We find that the value of the simplified derivative of S with respect to $C is $(-.462 \cdot \$C + \$15.78654)/[\$C^{.67} \cdot (\$68.34 - \$C)^{.67}]$. We next set this derivative or slope equal to zero to be at the point where S is a maximum at a total cost of $68.34. We then solve for $C in this equation. Doing so reveals that optimum $C = $-15.78654/-.462 = \$34.17$. For the final step, we plug this value of $C into the equation $68.34 = $L + $C, and then solve for $L. Doing so reveals that the optimum $L is also $34.17.

To determine the satisfaction level at this point, we palce the above benefit maximization values of $L and $C into the formula $S = .7 \cdot \sqrt{\$L} \cdot \sqrt{\$C}$, and we find that S = 7.37. Considering that the average S for the 49 agencies in the Auerbach data was only 6.45 with an average total cost of $68.34, this means that by properly allocating our total cost available to $L and $C, we can obtain an increase of .92 satisfaction units or 14% if the above satisfaction formula were real rather than hypothetical. The only binding constraint in this benefit maximization situation is the maximum total cost line. If it were raised, additional benefits could be had and opportunity costs avoided, but we do not know whether those additional satisfaction units would be worth the additional dollars.

In effect what we have done through this use of differential calculus is to find the value of $L and $C at the point where the highest possible satisfaction line just barely touches or is tangent to the maximum total cost line. As previously mentioned, this highest possible S line has a value of 7.37 at any point along the line. A satisfaction line .01 more than 7.37 (if the arithmetic is done accurately) would be beyond the capacity of a maximum total cost of $68.34 to reach. Likewise, a satisfaction line .01 unit less than 7.37 would be needlessly below the capacity of a maximum total cost of $68.34.

One might question the need for finding a derivative or slope, setting it equal to zero, and solving for $C (as we just did) when in this example one could have found that $C = $34.17 by merely dividing the $68.34 maximum cost by 2. This, however, is only true for this example because $L and $C are given the same cube root weights in the formula relating total benefits to $L and $C. In a less simple but more realistic example, $L and $C would have different weights and the exact optimum $L and $C for maximizing benefits on the maximum total cost line in Figure 6 could only be derived by consulting a table of derivatives and doing the algebra and arithmetic involved. One could, however, arrive at approximate optima for $L and $C by just observing where B seems to fall on a graph like Figure 6.

If spending the maximum total cost results in achieving more than the maximum total possible satisfaction, then one should find the value of $L and $C at the point where total costs are minimized at the 12.00 rather than 7.00 level of satisfaction. This involves going through the same steps described earlier for finding the value of $L and $C at a cost minimization point, by finding the derivative of the total cost with respect to $C for the equation TC = (5038/$C) + $C, setting that derivative equal to zero, solving for optimum $C, and then plugging that value back into the equation $12.00 = .7 \cdot \sqrt{\$L} \cdot \sqrt{\$C}$ to solve for optimum $L.

If more than two activity or independent variables are present in the nonlinear situation, and they cannot be meaningfully collapsed into two groups, then one should use a version of the above calculus approach which is known as partial differentiation or the use of partial derivatives. What that involves doing is finding the slope of the dependent, output, or goal variable with respect to the first activity variable while considering the other activity variables as if they were like numerical constants rather than variables. One then finds the slope of the objective function with respect to the second activity variable in the same way, and so on with each activity variable. Each of those separate slopes is then set to zero, providing as many equations as there are activity variables. One then solves for the numerical value of each activity variable the same way one solves for N unknowns where one has N equations. Those solutions should indicate the optimum allocations to each activity variable.[16]

In all the linear programming examples that we have used, the variables to which our scarce resources are to be allocated have been different activities, functions, or types of expenditures such as media versus canvassing activities, anti-government versus anti-private discrimination activities, or law reform versus case handling activities. Within social science problems, other entities to which scarce resources are allocated include geographical entities. For example, in an election campaign, how might a candidate best allocate his scarce funds among counties or other political units within his district? How might the NAACP allocate its scarce funds geographically among 50 states to fight discrimination? Likewise, how might the nationwide OEO Legal Services Program allocate its funds among its 250 or so local programs to maximize the total national satisfaction with the overall program? Questions like these can also be answered or at least approximated or further clarified through the use of the concepts and methods associated with linear programming (see Nagel and Neef, 1976d).[17]

III. INVENTORY MODELING AND OPTIMUM LEVEL ANALYSIS

In the optimum mix or linear programming perspective, we are primarily concerned with finding the optimum allocation or mix of scarce resources to two or more activities or other things in light of a given goal subject to various constraints. In the optimum level perspective, we are primarily concerned with finding the optimum quantity or level of an input in light of a given goal subject to various constraints. The optimum mix perspective thus involves two or more inputs, whereas the optimum level perspective basically involves only one input. Sometimes an optimum mix problem can be meaningfully translated into an optimum level problem where each of the multiple inputs can be expressed in terms of one input with each input having a turn at being that one input.

THE LINEAR SITUATION

The simplest type of optimum level problem is one in which the input variable bears a linear relation with the goal variable. The problem of free press versus fair trial with regard to the reporting of prejudicial pretrial publicity can be used to illustrate that situation. At first glance this free press versus fair trial problem looks like an optimum mix problem. It is, however, an optimum level problem because in this context freedom of the newspapers to report damaging information concerning pending criminal cases (FP) is by definition the complement of a fair trial that is free from having damaging information reported about a defendant in a pending criminal case (FT). Thus, if we can determine the optimum level of free press in pending criminal trials, then we have in effect determined the optimum level of fair trial in the same situation.[18]

In 1970, a national survey was made of newspaper editors, police chiefs, prosecuting attorneys, and defense attorneys from a sample of 166 cities across the country. The survey was designed to determine for each city how much free press was allowed in terms of the tendency of the newspapers to release various kinds of information concerning pending criminal cases. The survey was also designed to determine how much satisfaction each respondent felt with the practices that prevailed in his or her city. Through a kind of scalogramming methodology, it was determined that the free press scale had the following key points with regard to what kind of information was *not* allowed to be released by newspapers prior to trial: guilty plea bargaining (77%), opinions on case (74%), test results (65%), witness testimony (65%), statements by accused (64%), criminal record (50%), evidence seized at arrest (36%), details of arrest (13%), and name and charge (2%).

The information on the amount of satisfaction received by each respondent was fed into a regression analysis as the dependent variable along with information for each respondent on the amount of free press present in his city. The regression equation which resulted was $S = 60 + .30$ FP, where both satisfaction and free press were measured on a scale going from 0 to 100. Since fair trial is the complement of free press in this context, the regression equation between satisfaction and fair trial was $S = 60 + .30(100\text{-FT})$, or $S = 90 - .30$ FT.

Figure 7 shows these relations graphically. The figure also shows that the minimum fair trial allowed by the courts is about the 35 level. This was determined mainly on the basis of an analysis of the relevant court cases and the commentary literature after that verbal material was translated into points on the numerical scale. The maximum free press allowed is thus at the 65 level since free press is the scale complement of fair trial. Analysis of the same literature tends to indicate that the minimum free press constraint is at about the 50 level which means the maximum fair trial score is also at about the 50 level.

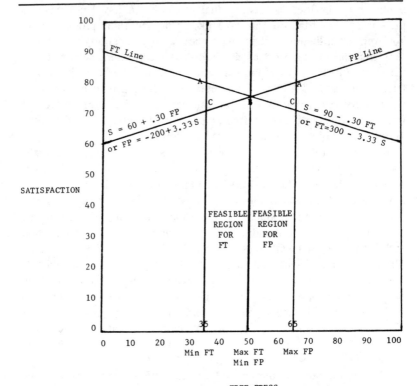

FREE PRESS
AND FAIR TRIAL

Point A is where free press is maximized and fair trial is minimized within the constraints. At that point, FP = 65, FT = 35, and S = 80.

Point B is where fair trial is maximized and free press is minimized within the constraints. At that point, FP = 50, FT = 50, and S = 75.

Point C is where free press and fair trial are in the average city in the survey. At that point, FP = 38, FT = 62, and S = 71.

Figure 7: Finding the Optimum Level of Free Press and Fair Trial to Maximize Satisfaction

Figure 7 further shows that as we go up on free press (toward the right on the FP line) or down on fair trial (toward the left on the FT line), we go up on satisfaction. We cannot, however, legally go up higher than a satisfaction score of 80 because to do so would involve going above the maximum free press constraint of 65 or below the minimum fair trial constraint of 35. Thus, the level of free press which gives the maximum satisfaction is the maximum free press obtainable without violating the legal constraints. At this level, it is permissible to publish pretrial information on matters as prejudicial as test results or witness testimony, but not as prejudicial as opinions on the case or information about guilty plea bargaining.

The data in Figure 7 is based on a regression analysis applied to all the respondents from the survey. A similar optimum level analysis can be applied to each occupational set within the respondents. Thus, we get a different regression equation if we only use the newspaper editors, namely a regression equation of $S = 21 + .82$ FP. For police chiefs, we get $S = 54 + .52$ FP. For prosecutors, we get $S = 63 + .32$ FP, and for defense attorneys, we get $S = 68 + .16$ FP. Notice that the weight of free press goes down as we move from newspaper editors to defense attorneys. In all four cases, however, the weight of free press is positive rather than negative, whereas it might have been negative if we had included criminal defendants. Thus, for all four types of occupations, the optimum level of free press is the maximum 65-level legally obtainable, although the amount of satisfaction received by each occupation varies at that level.

THE NONLINEAR SITUATION

Instead of feeding into the computerized linear regression analysis a satisfaction score and a free press score for each respondent, we could have fed in the logarithm of the satisfaction score and the logarithm of the free press score in order to obtain a nonlinear regression equation. Such a regression equation would read $S = 36(FP)^{.17}$, instead of $S = 60 + .30(FP)$. The nonlinear equation, however, does not account for substantially more of the variation on S among the respondents, and therefore the complications involved in working with it do not seem merited. The optimum FP would still be 65 although the total satisfaction at that point would be 74 rather than 80 due to diminishing returns.

The more interesting nonlinear situation is one in which the goal variable eventually curves downward as the input variable is increased rather than merely continuing to move upward at a diminishing rate. The optimum level of the input variable is then the point at which the goal variable reaches its peak on a hill-shaped benefit curve. Closely related is the situation in which the goal variable is a total cost variable which we are seeking to minimize, and in which that total cost variable goes down as the input variable is increased, but then eventually goes up. The optimum level of the input variable in that situation is the point at which the negative goal variable reaches its bottom on a U-shaped or valley-shaped cost curve.

The U-shaped total cost curve often exists in policy problems because as the input is increased, a certain type of cost goes up; but if the input is decreased, another type of cost goes up. The total cost curve is then the sum of the type one plus the type two costs. This is exactly what is involved in the inventory model problem which is probably the second most common operations research problem. It basically involves the fact that if a business firm carries inventories that are too large, there will be excessive storage and spoilage costs. On the other hand, if a business firm carries inventories that are too small, there will be excessive outage costs or lost sales due to lack of inventory. The object is to find the optimum inventory level where the sum of the holding or storage costs plus the releasing or outage costs is at a minimum.[19]

The Pretrial Release Problem

One political science example involving reasoning similar to the inventory model is the problem of the optimum percentage of defendants to hold in jail prior to trial, or the complementary problem of the optimum percentage of defendants to release prior to trial. If too many defendants are held, there will be the human analog of high storage and spoilage costs, but if too few defendants are held, there will be high releasing costs. Later, in section IV, we will discuss the problem of whether or not to release a given defendant in an individual case.

In 1969, questionnaires were mailed to judges, prosecutors, defense attorneys, and bail project directors in 80 cities. There was at least one respondent for each of the 72 cities. To illustrate the inventory model applied to the pretrial release problem, however, we will only use the 23 cities that provided complete information for all the basic variables. The basic variables for each city included:

(1) the number of defendants held in jail pending trial during 1968,

(2) the number of defendants released,

(3) the jail costs per day per inmate,

(4) the average number of days each inmate was held,

(5) the percent of defendants held in jail who were not subsequently found guilty,

(6) the percent of defendants released who failed to show up in court, and

(7) the percent of released defendants who were arrested for committing another crime while released.

From these basic variables, three holding costs were calculated on a per defendant basis for each city:

(1) total jail costs,

(2) total lost national income costs figured at an average monthly wage of $360 per month, and

(3) total bitterness costs figured at $300 per month of incarceration for each defendant not found guilty.[20]

From these basic variables, two releasing costs were also calculated:

(1) total rearrest costs figured at an average rearrest cost of $200 for those failing to show up in court, and

(2) total crime committing costs figured at an average cost of $1,000 for each defendant who committed a crime while released.[21]

For each of the 23 cities, we can plot a dot on a graph like Figure 8 showing the percent held or %H and the total *holding* costs. If we draw a smooth curved line through those 23 dots so as to minimize the sum of the distances squared from the dots to the line, we get a positive convex curve[22] like that shown in Figure 8. The equation for that curve is THC = $1185(\%H)^{1.31}$. Likewise, for each of the 23 cities, we can plot a dot showing the %H and the total *releasing* costs. If we draw a least-squares curved line through those 23 dots, we get a negative convex curve like that shown in Figure 8. The equation for that curve is TRC = $77(\%H)^{-.17}$ Since total costs are the sum of holding costs and releasing costs, we can show an asymmetrical valley-shaped total cost curve by adding

(1) the distance from the horizontal axis up to the THC curve and

(2) the distance from the horizontal axis up to the TRC curve, in order to create

(3) the TC curve.

The equation for that curve is TC = $1185(\%H)^{1.31} + 77(\%H)^{-.17}$ since TC = THC + TRC. In order to blow up the area of Figure 8 where the total cost curve reaches a bottom point, Figure 8 is not drawn exactly to scale. Also, if %H were allowed to go to 0% rather than 1% or .01 on the figure, then at that point TRC would equal infinity. At 1%, total holding costs equal $3, total releasing costs equal $168, and total costs equal $171.

What is the meaning of the shape of these curves? The total *holding cost* goes up as %H goes up, but more rapidly as %H gets higher. This is because the last defendants to be detained as %H approaches 100% would

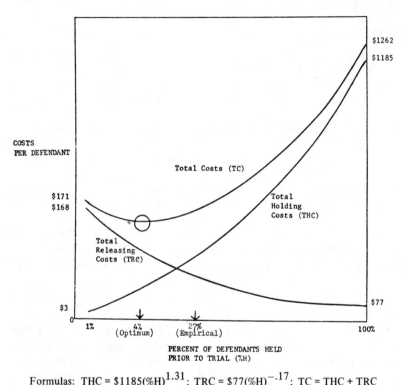

Formulas: THC = $\$1185(\%H)^{1.31}$; TRC = $\$77(\%H)^{-.17}$; TC = THC + TRC

Figure 8: The Holding, Releasing, and Total Bail Cost Curves for a Sample of 23 American Cities (not drawn to exact scale)

tend to be those who are most likely to be the best risk defendants and thus incur the highest holding costs with regard to

(1) lost national income since they are more likely to have steady, good-paying jobs,

(2) bitterness since they are the ones most likely to be acquitted, and

(3) expensive jail costs since they do jail time with relatively greater difficulty and thus require extra jail costs to care for them.

The total *releasing cost* goes up as %H goes down, but more rapidly as %H gets lower. This is because the last defendants to be released as %H approaches 0% would tend to be those who are most likely to be the worst risk defendants and thus incur the highest releasing costs with regard to

(1) rearrest costs for failing to show up in court and

(2) costs for committing crimes while released pending trial.

The total cost curve goes down as %H decreases from 0% to 4% and then the total cost curve goes up as %H increases from 4% to 100%. This is because before 4%, the TRC curve is falling faster than the THC curve is rising; whereas after 4%, the THC curve is rising faster than the TRC curve is falling. At 4%, the TRC curve is falling as fast as the THC curve is rising.

How do we know that total costs will bottom out at 4%? We could see that graphically with rough accuracy. For greater accuracy, what we need to do is find the value of %H when the slope, marginal change, or incremental change on the TC curve reaches 0. Prior to that bottom point, the slope of the TC curve is negative; and subsequent to that bottom point, the slope of the TC curve is positive. The slope of the TC curve is always the sum of the slope of the THC curve and the slope of the TRC curve. In elementary statistics or high school algebra, one learns that if there is a linear relationship between Y and X such that $Y = a + bX$, then the slope of Y with respect to X equals b, or $(Y_2 - Y_1)/(X_2 - X_1)$. Likewise, on a slightly more advanced level, if there is a nonlinear relationship between Y and X such that $Y = aX^b$, then the slope of Y with respect to X equals baX^{b-1}. Applying this rule to our equation for TC, we can say that the slope of TC with respect to %H equals $(1.31)(1185)(\%H)^{1.31-1.00} + (-.17)(77)(\%H)^{-.17-1.00}$. If we set that summation expression equal to 0 and then solve for %H, we find that the value of %H for that equation is .039505 or 4% as the optimum percentage of defendants to hold pending trial if one wants to minimize total costs as we have defined them in light of the empirical data we have. What we have done is analogous to what the rational business firm producing one product is supposed to do when it decides on an optimum level of goods to produce in order to maximize its total profits.

What happens to our 4% optimum if our releasing or holding costs were different from those provided by our sample or assumptions or if our costs were to change over time? Graphically, one can see that if the fixed holding costs go up, then the total holding costs curve will shift upward parallel to the former THC curve. The total cost curve will also rise upward, but its bottom point will still be above the 4% mark on the horizontal axis. On the other hand, if the THC curve remains anchored on the left at the zero origin point, and its slope changes as a result of a change in the variable holding costs which are influenced by the size of %H, then the optimum 4%

(1) will fall if THC goes up in order to offset the relatively higher holding costs, and

(2) will rise if THC goes down in order to offset the relatively higher releasing costs.

Likewise, if the TRC curve remains anchored in the lower right hand corner of the graph, and its slope changes as a result of a change in the releasing costs which are influenced by the size of %H, then the optimum 4%

(1) will fall if TRC goes down in order to benefit from the relatively lower releasing costs, and

(2) will rise if TRC goes up in order to benefit from the relatively lower holding costs.

For greater accuracy, these graphical relations can be reduced to algebraic equations. One useful equation is to know, as we previously indicated, that $\%H^*$ (or the optimum $\%H$) is the value of $\%H$ when one solves for $\%H$ in the equation) $= b_1 a_1 (\%H)^{b_1 - 1} + b_2 a_2 (\%H)^{b_2 - 1}$, where a_1 is the multiplier and b_1 is the exponent in the THC equation, and where a_2 is the multiplier and b_2 is the exponent in the TRC equation. Thus, to see how $\%H^*$ changes when there is a change in any of the costs, we can solve for $\%H^*_{t1}$ and $\%H^*_{t2}$, where $\%H^*_{t1}$ is the optimum $\%H$ at the time 1 based on the first set of costs, multipliers, and exponents as determined by the least-squares line and solving for $\%H$, and where $\%H^*_{t2}$ is the optimum $\%H$ at time 2 based on the second set of costs, multipliers, and exponents as similarly determined.

How can we individualize on a per city basis our general finding that the optimum percent of defendants to hold pending trial is approximately 4% working with our sample of 23 cities? One approach we can use is to divide the sample into metropolitan, urban, and rural cities, and then recalculate the optimum percent for each of these three subsamples. Doing so still produces an optimum of about 4% for each subsample although holding costs and releasing costs are both higher in larger cities. If both those costs rise or fall together, however, they tend to offset each other, leaving the optimum percent about the same. We could calculate a separate optimum percent for each city if we could get data at more than one time point for each city, or else apply the average optimum of 4% to each city. Even with data for only one time point, we can still roughly create an individualized THC curve and TRC curve for each city by assuming the THC curve has the quadratic form THC $= a_1 (\%H)^2$, and the TRC curve has the rectangular hyperbolic form TRC $= a_2 (\%H)^{-1}$. We can then solve for the value of a_1 for any city by plugging its THC and %H score into the first equation, and solve for the value of a_2 for any city by plugging its TRC and %H score into the second equation.[23] Thus, knowing a_1 and

a_2, we can solve for $\%H^*$ for any city by solving for $\%H$ in the equation $0 = 2a_1(\%H)^{2-1} + -1a_2(\%H)^{-1-1}$, which means $\%H^*$ for any given city under these assumptions equals the cube root of $(a_2/2a_1)$.

Closely related to the analysis of variations on the model is the causal implications problem of how to explain why the optimum level is 4% when the empirical reality for the 23 cities was an average of 27% of defendants held in jail pending trial. That discrepancy can be explained by a variety of factors. Perhaps we have excluded some releasing costs that arraignment judges include which might raise the 4%, such as the opportunity which is lost by releasing a defendant when pretrial detention could have been used as a deterrent form of punishment, although we have simultaneously excluded some holding costs which might lower the 4% such as the costs of convicting innocent defendants, jail riots, and damage to the family of a defendant. Perhaps we have also wrongly included some holding costs that arraignment judges exclude or include less than we have done, such as the loss of national income, although arraignment judges probably do consider middle class defendants to be better risks. Perhaps the discrepancy might be partly due to arraignment judges overly misperceiving the likelihood that defendants will fail to show up or will commit crimes while released. We could change our cost considerations to try to make the optimum rise closer to the empirical so that the new optimum might more accurately reflect the motives of arraignment judges, or we could recommend that arraignment judges release more defendants in order to get the empirical down closer to the optimum.

That kind of analysis logically leads to the further policy implications of the model. Perhaps the most important policy implication is to point up the need to release more defendants pending trial in order to minimize the total social costs involved in the pretrial release process. It is logical to ask how one determines what defendants go into the 4% to be held and what defendants go into the 96% to be released. The problem of discriminating between those to be held and those to be released can be handled by developing point systems comparable to those used by the Vera Foundation in New York City. One difficult aspect of such a point system is determining the cutoff threshold above which one is released and below which one is detained. If it has been determined that only the worst 4% should be detained, then one could determine what scores were made by the lowest 4% in a large sample of defendants. That range of scores would indicate the cutoff threshold to be used in future cases. The Vera approach is helpful for scoring the future cases, and the optimizing approach is helpful for indicating where the cutoff score ought to be. The two approaches dovetail even better if they consider directly or indirectly roughly the same criteria in arriving at their conclusions. Another set of policy implications relates to the problem of how to reduce the total costs of the pre-trial release process besides simply changing the empirical percentage held in a city up to or down to the city's optimum percentage. The total costs can be reduced by reducing the total *holding costs* which are largely determined by the average jail length, which in turn can be reduced by the efforts directed toward reduction of case load, case processing time, and lack of judge time. The total costs can also be reduced by reducing the total *releasing costs* which are largely determined by the percent of defend-ants who commit crimes while released, which in turn can be reduced by better screening techniques, shorter release time until trial, and various anti-crime efforts.

Other Political-Legal Policy Applications

Perhaps the most important potential contribution of a study of the methodological, causal, and policy implications of the problem of mini-mizing total costs for pretrial release or total costs in inventory lot size is the potential applicability of the model to a wide variety of legal policy problems. These legal policy problems could conceivably include how far to go in providing certain aspects of due process in criminal and civil cases, how severe various regulatory or other laws should be, and how many cases should be scheduled per day in a judicial or quasi-judicial system.

By model in this context is meant a system of three equations in which one equation is a rising-cost equation of the form $TCP = a_1(P)^{b_1}$, where P = the degree of effort expended in pursuing a policy; TCP = the total cost of pursuing the policy; a = amount of TCP incurred if one unit of effort is expended in pursuing the policy; and b_1 = a positive number to which P is raised to show the degree of increasing TCP costs from addition-al units of P. In our bail example, TCP = THC, and P = %H.

The second equation is a falling cost equation (with regard to the same policy problem) of the form $TCQ = a_2(P)^{b_2}$, where TCQ = the total cost of pursuing the opposite of the policy; a_2 = amount of TCQ incurred if one uint of effort is expended in pursuing the policy; and b_2 = a negative number to which P is raised to show the degree of falling TCQ costs from additional units of P. In our bail example, TCQ = TRC. The third equation is a total cost equation that represents the sum of the left sides of the first two equations and has the form TC = TCP + TCQ, where TC = total costs of pursuing a policy which incurs relatively high costs if too little or too much of the policy is pursued. The object of the model is to find the value of P where TC is at a minimum.

We would have the same model if the equations were production functions rather than cost functions of the form $TBP = a_1(P)^{b_1}$, $TBQ = a_2(P)^{b_2}$, and $TB = TBP + TBQ$, where TB = total benefits of pursuing a policy which incurs relatively low benefits if too little or too much of the policy is pursued. The object then is to find the value of P where TB is at a maximum. Likewise, we still have the same nonlinear summation optimization model if we combine costs and benefits. For example, we might want to maximize net benefits or profits where $NB = TBQ - TCQ$ or $NB = TBP - TCP$. It is, however, usually easier algebraically and geometrically to think of minimizing TC or maximizing TB rather than maximizing NB even through each of these three formulations can be translated into the other.[24]

The model can also be defined geometrically as shown in Figure 9, especially Figure 9c. There we have our familiar intersecting convex cost curves which create the U-shaped or valley-shaped total cost curves. In the figure, for simplicity both convex cost curves have the same slope, meaning that the minimum point on TC is at the point of intersection. That simplification is not necessary to the generalized model as shown back in Figure 8. Likewise, in Figure 9 all the cost curves end at the horizontal axis, meaning there are no fixed costs, but that also is not necessary to the generalized model. Furthermore, in spite of Figure 8, the generalized model does not require that TRC be on the left as a falling cost curve and THC be on the right as a rising cost curve. We can easily reverse the left-right positions of the TRC and THC curves by simply redefining the policy variable as being the percent to release rather than as being the percent to hold.[25] The way such a policy variable is stated is purely arbitrary, although sometimes one version may be preferred over the other because that version sounds more positive or more customary.[26]

Figure 9A applies the model to the most important problem in legal procedure, namely how much due process should be provided in criminal and civil cases. The figure specifically deals with criminal cases, but would be applicable to civil cases if we talk in terms of the cost of finding non-wrongdoers to be liable and the cost of finding wrongdoers to be non-liable. By due process, Figure 9A means procedural matters like providing free counsel to defendants, excluding illegally obtained evidence, and providing jury trials. The figure indicates that the more due process we have—with regard to any of these components or all of them collectively on a scale from 0 to 100—the more releasing costs we will incur by acquitting guilty persons. Likewise, the less due process we have, the more holding costs we will incur by convicting and jailing innocent persons.

A. DUE PROCESS AND ERROR COSTS

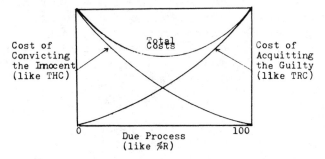

Cost of
Convicting
the Innocent
(like THC)

Total
Costs

Cost of
Acquitting
the Guilty
(like TRC)

0   100

Due Process
(like %R)

B. LAW SEVERITY AND ERROR COSTS

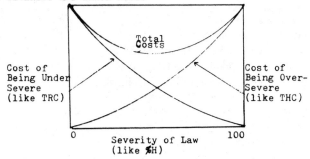

Cost of
Being Under
Severe
(like TRC)

Total
Costs

Cost of
Being Over-
Severe
(like THC)

0   100

Severity of Law
(like %H)

C. THE MODEL GENERALIZED

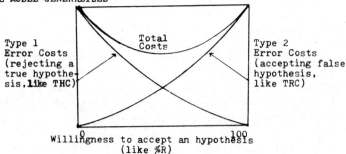

Type 1
Error Costs
(rejecting a
true hypothe-
sis, like THC)

Total
Costs

Type 2
Error Costs
(accepting false
hypothesis,
like TRC)

0   100

Willingness to accept an hypothesis
(like %R)

Figure 9: Graphing the Relations Between Legal Policies and Error Costs

The difficult problem in this (or any kind of) policy analysis is in measuring the relevant variables. It is, however, not too difficult to determine how readily available jury trials, free legal counsel, or other due process procedures are in a sample of cities or states. The availability of these procedures could be expressed as percentages of a set of cases or as verbal categories on a high, medium, or low scale. What is more difficult is to get people knowledgeable about the criminal justice process in each of those places to say meaningful things about what percent of the cases involve convicting the guilty, acquitting the innocent, convicting the innocent, and acquitting the guilty. If one accepts that appellate courts are right when they reverse trial courts, one could do an analysis of affirmances and reversals for each state to see what percent of the appellate court cases involved reversing convictions, affirming convictions, reversing acquittals, and affirming acquittals. Since acquittals do not get appealed in view of the double jeopardy clause, one might be forced to use the above research design only with civil or personal injury cases where the appellate court set would be divided into reversals of plaintiff judgments, reversals of defendant judgments, affirmances of plaintiff judgments, and affirmances of defendant judgments. Any referral is an error cost either of type one (where the trial court judge erred in rejecting the prodefendant presumption) or type two (where the trial court judge erred in accepting the prodefendant presumption). After determining how often type one and type two errors occur, we still have to assign costs to them. The costs in personal injury cases can consist of the dollars wrongly awarded or wrongly withheld, but the costs are more difficult to assess in criminal cases.[27]

Figure 9B applies the model to the most (or at least one of the most) important problems in legal substance, namely how severe regulatory or other laws should be. This is a common model for analyzing the problem of how severe antipollution laws should be. In that context, the policy variable on the horizontal axis might be water cleanliness. To get 100% water cleanliness involves tremendous costs that rapidly rise as one moves from the easy to clean water to the more difficult water pollution problems. If one moves in the opposite direction toward zero percent cleanliness, the cleanup costs fall, but the pollution damage costs begin to rise rapidly especially when at zero cleanliness we may be plagued with typhoid epidemics and the like. Such a model enables one to decide better such water quality policy issues as the following:

(1) Where should the vertical constraint lines be with regard to how much cleanliness must be achieved by 1983, 1985, or other points in time? Such a line would be a minimum constraint line making

the area to the right of the line a feasible region and the area to the left of the line out of bounds.

(2) Where should the horizontal constraint lines be with regard to how much total cost our society is willing to bear in the water quality field as of 1983, 1985, or other points in time? Such a line would be a maximum constraint line, making the area below it a feasible region and the area above it out of bounds.

(3) Should the objective be to achieve the minimum point on the total cost curve as much within the constraints as possible, or to achieve the maximum water quality which would involve going as high on the rising cost curve as the constraints allow?

(4) How should the constraints differ for different levels of government, different industries, or different regions?

(5) In measuring cleanliness along the horizontal axis, should we measure the cleanliness of bodies of water like rivers and lakes, or should we measure the effluence from sources which enter into the bodies of water?

(6) What costs should we consider in determining the damage costs or the costs of not achieving clean water? Should these costs include aesthetics costs as well as damage to the fishing industry, public health, and recreation?

(7) What costs should we consider in determining the cleanup costs? Should we include possible secondary costs like reduced availability of atomic energy plants, increased unemployment, and increased consumer prices?

(8) How can we obtain relevant data and assess the above costs?

(9) If we are going to talk in terms of cleanliness of effluence rather than cleanliness of bodies of water, does effluence include smokestacks which emit pollutants that become part of the rainwater that falls on rivers and lakes? [28]

Although Figure 9B may be specially applicable to analyzing how severe economic regulatory laws should be, it is aslo applicable to a variety of basic common law problems in contracts, property, torts, and family law. For example, how severe or lenient should divorce laws be? If they are too severe in not allowing divorces, there will be high holding costs in forcing incompatible spouses to hold together—to the detriment of themselves, their children, and society. On the other hand, if the divorce laws are too lenient, there will be high releasing costs in allowing or even encouraging compatible spouses to break apart—to the detriment of themselves, their children, and society. Likewise, how severe should property laws be in seeking to compel landlords to conform to housing codes? How severe should sales contract laws be in seeking to compel merchants to conform to consumer codes? These problems involve costs analogous to holding costs and releasing costs, and they involve methodological considerations of varying degrees of difficulty with regard to assessing those costs for different places or times with different policies.

The inventory-type model is also applicable to problems that do not involve questions of due process or law severity. For example, the model nicely applies to the operations research problem of how many cases to schedule per day in a judicial or quasi-judicial system. If too many cases are scheduled, then releasing costs will be suffered, in the sense that people who have shown up for court will have to be released after having wasted time without compensating satisfaction. If too few cases are scheduled, holding costs will be suffered, in the sense that judges and other court personnel may be held in court without adequate work to do. For this problem, relevant cost and other data is now available in many court systems through their modern computerized time records. Instead of data for a set of different places as in the bail problem, those records enable one to work with data over many different points in time when different quantities of cases were scheduled (Jennings, 1971; Programming Methods, 1971).

The case scheduling problem also applies to scheduling potential jurors to come to the courthouse. If too many jurors are asked to come, then many potential jurors will have to be released after having spent time in a useless, frustrating way. If, on the other hand, too few jurors are asked to come, then holding costs will be suffered in the sense that judges and other court personnel may be held in court without being able to proceed with jury trials they could have processed. Both the case scheduling and the juror scheduling problem involve finding an optimum number of cases or number of jurors so as to minimize total costs, bearing in mind that wasted judge time may be more expensive than wasted lawyer time or wasted juror time (Merrill and Schrage, 1969; Pabst, 1973).

Figure 9C provides a generalized version of the model which is not tied to any legal policy problem or other policy problem. That figure involves a decision with regard to how willing we should be to accept a hypothesis. The hypothesis might be that defendants are innocent until proven guilty and therefore should be released pending trial; or the hypothesis might be any other legal presumption, or simply that the status quo should be preserved, or any other hypothesis. Accepting a false hypothesis involves type two error costs. An example is releasing a defendant who fails to show up for trial or who comits a crime while awaiting trial. Rejecting a true hypothesis involves type one error costs. An example is holding a defendant who would have shown up for a trial and would not have committed a crime, but who has incurred jail costs, lost GNP, and bitterness costs. These two types of costs and their components cover all the possible costs and indirectly the complementary benefits that are a function of one's willingness to accept a hypothesis. The costs can include intangible costs as well as monetary costs, but some common unit of measurement is needed in order to be able to sum them to determine meaningfully the total cost curve and the point or region where it reaches a minimum.

The cost or benefit curves and their respective equations can be arrived at by:

(1) using statistical induction to generalize a curve from data obtained for many firms, government agencies, places, or time points;

(2) relying on an awareness of how similar curves normally respond to changes in inputs; or

(3) deductively or mathematically analyzing accounting, engineering, or other technical information generally from a single firm, agency, place, or time point. [29]

The first method is illustrated by the regression analysis used in the previous section to arrive at $THC = 1185(\%H)^{1.31}$ and $TRC = 77(\%H)^{-.17}$. The second method is illustrated in the discussion of holding costs for individual cities based on the assumption that the curves approximate an increasing-costs quadratic curve of the form $THC = a(\%H)^2$ and a decreasing-costs rectangular hyperbolic curve of the form $TRC = a(\%H)^{-1}$. The third method is illustrated by the way cost curves can be arrived at in determining the optimum inventory size (X) for business firms. In that context, $THC = (UHC/2)(X)^1$ and $TRC = (URC \cdot Sales)(X)^{-1}$, where the unit holding cost (UHC), the unit releasing or outage cost (URC), and the sales per time period are arrived at through accounting information rather than through statistical regression analysis. [30] In all three situations, the optimum %H or X is found by finding the slope of TC with respect to %H or X, setting that slope to 0, and then solving for %H or X.

An appropriate name is needed for our generalized model in order to capture succinctly its essential characteristics. It is a nonlinear summation optimization model. It is nonlinear in the sense that it applies to policy problems in which the total costs or total benefits produced by varying degrees of the policy are valley-shaped or hill-shaped respectively. It is a summation model in the sense that the total costs are determined by summing a falling cost curve and a rising cost curve, and the total benefits are determined by summing a falling benefit curve and a rising benefit curve. The cost curves are generally convex, and the benefit curves are generally concave to reflect the almost universal phenomena of rising costs and diminishing returns respectively. The model is an optimization model in that it is primarily designed to arrive at an optimum policy position, although the model may also be quite useful in generating a better causal understanding of the relations among the variables. Unfortunately, the expression "nonlinear summation optimization model" is rather lengthy although it could be abbreviated to the NSO model. For a shorter although less fully descriptive expression, the model should possibly be referred to as "the error model" because in its most generalized form it enables one to think about what is involved in minimizing total error costs which equal the sum of type one error costs and type two error costs. It can also be referred to as the inventory model in light of its most frequent application in operations research.

IV. DECISION THEORY AND DYNAMIC EQUILIBRIUM ANALYSIS

As mentioned in the first section of this paper, the essence of decision theory as an optimizing tool is its handling of optimizing problems where what to do is contingent on the occurrence of uncertain events. In deciding the optimum choice among alternative decisions, we should take into consideration the probability that the key uncertain events will or will not occur.

The inventory model, for example, can be made more realistic by taking into consideration the fact that the sales per time period is a probabilistic occurrence rather than a deterministic one. This means that how high sales will be in any given period is not definite, but one can arrive at a probability figure to multiply sales by on the basis of past experience. Many of the variables in the bail problem could also be stated in probabilistic terms where the probabilities relate to the percent of released defendants who commit crimes while released, and the percent of held defendants who are not found guilty. We could then talk in terms of minimizing the total expected costs in light of the expected holding costs and expected releasing costs.[31]

THE ONE-PERSON DECISION SITUATION

The notion of probability is especially relevant in deciding whether or not to release a given defendant prior to trial in an individual case. That decision to release is an especially good decision problem to illustrate the one-person decision situation if we work, at least at first, with the simple question of whether to release or hold a given defendant, rather than the more complicated decision of how high the bail bond deposit should be set and the effect of the bond on the probability of appearing. The decision to release a defendant on his own recognizance (ROR) or to set bond low relative to the defendant's ability to pay is in effect a decision to release, whereas the decision to label a case a "no bond allowed" case or to set bond high relative to the defendant's ability to pay is in effect a decision to hold.[32]

Figure 10 shows the payoff matrices for two hypothetical judges in the same case. In that case, there are two alternative decisions available, namely release or hold. There are likewise two alternative categories on the contingent event:

(1) the defendant would appear if released, or

(2) the defendant would fail to appear if released.

The cells indicate the relative satisfaction or dissatisfaction received by each judge if he releases the defendant who then fails to appear (cell a); if he releases the defendant who does appear (cell b); if he holds the defendant when he would have failed to appear if released (cell c); and if he holds the defendant when he would have appeared if released (cell d).[33] The most satisfying occurrence is anchored at +100, and the most dissatisfying is anchored at −100.

The judge in Figure 10A is more concerned about holding a good-risk defendant than releasing a bad-risk defendant as indicated by the fact that he gets the most dissatisfaction from cell d. On the other hand, the judge in Figure 10B is more concerned about releasing a bad-risk defendant than holding a good-risk defendant, as indicated by the fact that he gets the most dissatisfaction from cell a. We assume that both judges are hearing the same case in the same city so that the differences in their perceived payoff values reflect their attitudinal differences. Otherwise, the differences might reflect the severity of the defendant's criminal behavior since the same judge could have a payoff matrix like 10B for a homocidal maniac, but a payoff matrix like 10A for a jaywalker. Likewise, a judge in a city that has high holding costs relative to releasing costs might have a payoff matrix like 10A, but a judge in a city that has high releasing costs relative to holding costs might have a payoff matrix like 10B. Holding costs in this context might refer to jail upkeep, lost earnings, and frequent bitterness due to misarrests, whereas releasing costs refer to the costs due to rearresting no-shows and the monetary and psychological costs of crimes committed by released defendants.

Suppose both judges perceived the defendant as having a probability of appearing (or PA) of about .60. If either judge were to be confronted with 10 such defendants, this means about six would appear for their trial date and four would fail to appear. If the same defendant were to be given 10 op-

10A. A JUDGE WHO IS MORE WORRIED ABOUT HOLDING A GOOD-RISK DEFENDANT THAN
RELEASING A BAD-RISK DEFENDANT

		PROBABILITY OF APPEARANCE (PA)		EXPECTED VALUE IF PA = .6
		Would Fail to Appear	Would Appear	
ALTERNATIVE DECISIONS AVAILABLE	Release via ROR or Low Bond	a −50	b +100	$(.4)(-50) + (.6)(+100) = +40$
	Hold via No or High Bond	c +75	d −100	$(.4)(+75) + (.6)(-100) = -30$

10B. A JUDGE WHO IS MORE WORRIED ABOUT RELEASING A BAD-RISK DEFENDANT THAN
HOLDING A GOOD-RISK DEFENDANT

		PROBABILITY OF APPEARANCE (PA)		EXPECTED VALUE IF PA = .6
		Would Fail to Appear	Would Appear	
ALTERNATIVE DECISIONS AVAILABLE	Release via ROR or Low Bond	a −100	b +25	$(.4)(-100) + (.6)(+25) = -25$
	Hold via No or High Bond	c +100	d −10	$(.4)(+100) + (.6)(-10) = +34$

Cells indicate relative satisfaction of each
occurrence with the most satisfying anchored at
+100 and the most dissatisfying anchored at -100.

**Figure 10: Decision Theory Payoff Matrices as Perceived by Two Arraignment
Judges Deciding Whether or Not to Release a Defendant**

portunities, this means he would appear about six times and he would fail
to appear four times. Thus, the expected values for judge 10A of releasing
10 such defendants would be: four times he would suffer a −50 dissatisfaction; six times he would receive a +100 satisfaction; and he would thus
average a +40 expected value from releasing our hypothetical defendant.
Likewise, the expected values for judge 10A of holding 10 such defendants
would be: four times he would receive a +75 satisfaction; six times he
would suffer a −100 dissatisfaction; and he would thus average a −30 expected value from holding our hypothetical defendant, assuming in both
the releasing and holding situation that he could be made aware of the

consequences of his actions. The same kind of expected value calculations could be done with judge 10B.

Given the logical assumption that any judge or any person will choose the action or alternative decision that gives him the highest expected value, judge 10A will logically release the hypothetical defendant with a PA of .60 and judge 10B will hold the hypothetical defendant. Rather than ask whether a given judge will release or hold a given defendant, the more interesting question is what is the threshold probability of appearance (or PA*) that has to be met before judge 10A or 10B will release a defendant. To calculate PA* for either judge, all we have to do is solve for PA in the equation $(1-PA)(a) + (PA)b = (1-PA)(c) + (PA)(d)$ since at that PA level, the expected value of releasing exactly equals the expected value of holding. Thus, for judge 10A, his PA* equals .385; whereas for judge 10B, his PA* equals .851. This means judge 10A will release (or should release if he wants to maximize his expected values) any defendant who has a .39 or higher chance of appearing, and will hold any defendant who has a .38 or lower chance of appearing. On the other hand, judge 10B will release (or should release if he wants to maximize his expected values) any defendant who has a .86 or higher chance of appearing, and will hold any defendant who has a .85 or lower chance of appearing. Judge 10A probably releases a substantially higher percentage of the defendants who appear before him than judge 10B does if their judicial behavior reflects their differential values and they face roughly the same defendants.

The above analysis logically leads to perceiving how a judge seeking to optimize his values might set bond. First such a judge would determine his PA* threshold. Then he would determine whether the defendant's probability of appearing (PA) is greater than PA* regardless of the bond set. If so, the defendant can be released on his own recognizance or on a nominal bond. If not, bond should be set high enough to bring the defendant's PA up above PA*. If no bond can do that, then the defendant may have to be held in jail pending a speedy trial. If the bond that can do that (that is, bring PA above PA*) is too high for the defendant to meet, then he may also have to be held while awaiting trial.

Some interesting policy and theory questions that this kind of analysis might raise and help answer include: if we ask a set of arraignment judges to indicate their values in a payoff matrix like those shown in Figure 10, what variables might explain why some judges have a higher PA* threshold than other judges do? If some set of policy-makers like a state legislature or a state supreme court decides the proper PA* threshold should be .5 or should be the average that prevails among the judges in a given city or a state, then how can we get individual judges to move down or up to that threshold? What might be the effect of showing the judges how their value orientations compare anonymously with each other analogous to the way sentencing disparity seminars sometimes operate in order to reduce sentencing disparities? How can other criteria besides PA be considered in the model? How can nondiscretionary bond-amount schedules or charts be most rationally determined whereby fixed bonds are assigned to various crimes?

THE TWO-PERSON BARGAINING SITUATION

The pretrial release problem just presented involves a decision-maker seeking to maximize or optimize certain goals irrespective of the decisions made by another person who is seeking to gain at the expense of our decision-maker. We presented two judges to illustrate the methodology, but those two judges do not interact with each other in conflict or cooperation in the model in determining the outcomes of individual cases, although the judicial system might like to see judges cooperate with each other more in order to reduce disparities in their bond-setting practices. In setting bond in the model, the judge also generally does not haggle with the defendant, although the judicial system might like to see more interaction there in order to enable the judge to obtain information whereby he could more meaningfully individualize his bond-setting. Unlike this pretrial release model, any model of the bargaining between the prosecutor and the defendant or his defense counsel over the charge or sentence to be given in return for a plea of guilty would have to involve an interactive decision-making situation. Such a plea bargaining situation can be used to illustrate some of the basic concepts and methods involved in operations research applied to the two-person bargaining situation.

The Basic Model

Figure 11 provides a time path graph of the plea bargaining process. A time path graph is a graph that shows how converging or diverging variables change over time. The horizontal axis shows time points in the plea bargaining process from the initial offer (time point 0) to the first counteroffer (time point 1) to convergence or equilibrium (which in this hypothetical case is at time point 4). The vertical axis shows the years offered (or charges converted into years) by the defendant and the prosecutor at the different stages, steps, or time points in the plea bargaining process. [34]

Important matters to note for now which will be clarified shortly include the fact that the adjusted maximum bargaining limit of the defendant-buyer (ALD) is about 5-1/2 years, and the adjusted minimum

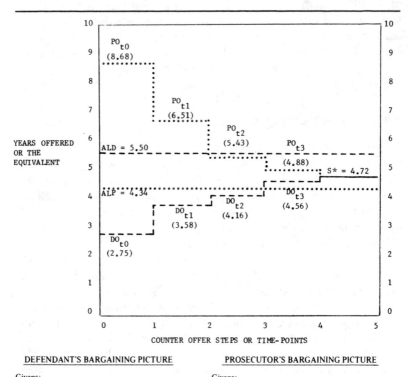

DEFENDANT'S BARGAINING PICTURE

Givens:

   a = 4, b = 7, c = 0, d = 10, PC = .5,
   %XD = .10, EF = .5, RD = .3

Calculations:

   $LS_1 = (1 - PC)c + (PC)d = 5$
   $LS_2 = (1 - PC)a + (PC)b = 5.5$
   LD = LS_1 or LS_2, whichever lower = 5
   $ALD = LD + (\%XD \cdot LD) = 5 + (.10 \cdot 5) = 5.5$
   $O_{t0} = EF \cdot ALD = .5(5.5) = 2.75$
   $O_{t1} = O_{t0} + RD(ALD - O_{t0})$
         $= 2.75 + .3(5.5 - 2.75) = 3.58$

PROSECUTOR'S BARGAINING PICTURE

Givens:

   a = 3, b = 6, c = 0, d = 8, PC = .7,
   %XP = .15, EF = 2, RP = .5

Calculations:

   $LS_1 = (1 - PC)c + (PC)d = 5.6$
   $LS_2 = (1 - PC)a + (PC)b = 5.1$
   LP = LS_1 or LS_2, whichever lower = 5.1
   $ALP = LP - (\%XP \cdot LP) = 5.1 - (.15 \cdot 5.1) = 4.34$
   $O_{t0} = EF \cdot ALP = 2(4.34) = 8.68$
   $O_{t1} = O_{t0} - RP(O_{t0} - ALP)$
         $= 8.68 - .5(8.68 - 4.34) = 6.51$

See text for definitions.

Figure 11: A Time Path Graph of Plea Bargaining from Initial Offers to Counteroffers to Equilibrium

bargaining limit of the prosecutor-seller (ALP) is about 4-1/3 years. The defendant's initial offer at time 0 is about 2-3/4 years (DO_{t0}), and the prosecutor's initial offer is about 8-2/3 years (PO_{t0}). The defendant proceeds upward in ascending staircase fashion toward his limit of 5.50, and the prosecutor proceeds downward in descending staircase fashion toward his limit of 4.34. They converge or settle at 4.72 years where the defendant feels he has gained something since he was willing to go as high as 5.50, and the prosecutor feels he has gained something since he was willing to go as low as 4.34.

In order to clarify this hypothetical time path graph, we might start by first answering the question: how did we arrive at the defendant's maximum bargaining limit of 5.50 and the prosecutor's minimum bargaining limit of 4.34? The answer is provided by the hypothetical payoff data shown in Figure 12. The figure shows that our hypothetical defendant or his attorney perceives the probability of a conviction as being .5, whereas our hypothetical prosecutor perceives the probability of a conviction as being .7. Our defendant further perceives that:

(1) if he is *acquitted* on trial (cell c), he will receive 0 years;

(2) if he is *convicted* on trial (cell d), he will receive 10 years;

(3) If he goes before a judge with a non-negotiated guilty plea when he would have been acquitted for lack of admissible incriminating evidence (cell a), he will receive 4 years; and

(4) if he pleads guilty in a non-negotiated plea when he would have been convicted (cell b), he will receive 7 years.

For the same four cells, our prosecutor perceives the sentence payoffs to be 0, 8, 3, and 6 respectively. The hypothetical data is realistic with regard to the fact that:

(1) sentences on pleading guilty are normally less than sentences on trial conviction when the crime is held constant, and

(2) sentences with less incriminating evidence are normally less than sentences with more incriminating evidence when other matters are also held constant.

Given the data in cells a and b of the defendant's payoff matrix, the expected value or best sentence estimate to the defendant from making a non-negotiated guilty plea is about 5½ years. That value is in effect an arithmetic mean of the 4 and 7 scores weighted by the .5 perceived probability of the 4 score and the .5 perceived probability of the 7 score. Likewise, given the data in cells c and d of the defendant's payoff matrix, the expected sentence from going to trial is about 5 years. Thus, if the defendant were only interested in minimizing his sentence, he should be pleased to accept any offer from the prosecutor that involves *less* than a 5-year sentence since the defendant's best fallback position is 5 years. This is what we mean by the unadjusted limit or LD of the defendant. Similar calculations can be made for the prosecutor's payoff matrix.

12A. A DEFENDANT'S PAYOFF MATRIX

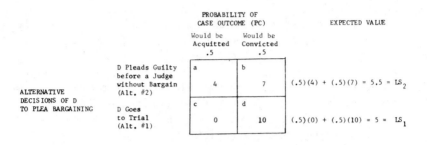

Cells indicate likely sentences (LS) in years
as perceived by a hypothetical defendant (D).

12B. A PROSECUTOR'S PAYOFF MATRIX

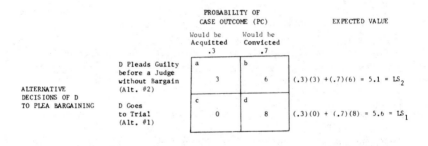

Cells indicate likely sentences (LS) in years
as perceived by a hypothetical prosecutor (P).

Figure 12: Payoff Matrices as Perceived by a Defendant and a Prosecutor in a Hypothetical Felony Case

Doing so would indicate that if the prosecutor were only interested in maximizing the sentence, he should be glad to accept any offer from the defendant that involves *more* than a 5.1 year sentence since that is the worst position that the prosecutor perceives the defendant can fall back to if negotiations break down (that is, worst from the prosecutor's point of view). Thus, 5.1 is the prosecutor's unadjusted limit or LP.

To adjust the defendant's limit for nonsentence goals, it is usually necessary to add a bonus factor or XD to LD. This bonus factor reflects the fact that the defendant-buyer is willing to give the prosecutor-seller a bonus for early resolution of the transaction in order to avoid such possible litigation costs as the cost of staying in jail awaiting trial, the cost of hiring a trial attorney, and the cost in time, anxieties, and damage to reputation. These litigation costs, however, are partly offset by such settlement costs as the possible early loss of the defendant's freedom, the waiver of the safeguards associated with a jury trial, and the possibility that with delay witnesses might forget or become unavailable. In our hypothetical data, we use a defendant whose bonus percentage or %XD is 10%. Thus, his adjusted limit is 5 years *plus* 10% of 5 years which sums to 5½ years. To adjust the prosecutor's limit for nonsentence goals, it is usually necessary to subtract a discount factor or XP from LP. This discount factor reflects the fact that the prosecutor-seller is willing to give the defendant-buyer a discount for early resolution of the transaction in order to

(1) save the costs of preparing for a trial and appearing in court,

(2) reduce the backlog of cases awaiting trial, and sometimes

(3) to obtain cooperation from the defendant as a witness or informer in other cases.

These litigation costs which encourage settlement, however, are partly offset by such settlement costs as the loss of publicity from a trial where the prosecutor may be politically motivated or may be seeking to use the defendant as an example to others, even though the likely sentence from the trial might be less than what the prosecutor could achieve through plea bargaining. In our illustrative hypothetical data we use a prosecutor whose discount percentage or %XP is 15%. Thus, his adjusted limit is 5.1 years *minus* 15% of 5.1 years which leaves a remainder of 4.34 or about 4-1/3 years.

The defendant's initial offer or O_{t0} equals his adjusted limit (or ALD) times an exaggeration factor which is a decimal less than one. His exaggeration factor is largely determined by his bluffing psychology rather than by any mathematical modeling. For illustration purposes, we assume an exaggeration factor of .5, meaning the defendant's initial offer will be half of 5.50 which yields an initial offer of 2.75 or about 2-3/4 years. The prosecutor's initial offer equals his adjusted limit (or ALP) times an exaggeration factor which is a number greater than one. If we assume an exaggeration factor for the prosecutor of 2.0, then the prosecutor's initial offer will be double 4.34 which yields an initial offer of 8.68 or about 8-2/3 years. Each successive offer of the defendant involves splitting the remaining distance between his relatively low previous offer and his upper limit at a constant or nonconstant splitting rate. If we assume a constant splitting rate or RD of .3, then the defendant's first counteroffer or O_{t1} will be 2.75 *plus* .3 of the remaining difference between 2.75 and his maximum limit of 5.5, which yields a first counteroffer of 3.58 or about 3½ years. Each successive offer of the prosecutor involves splitting the remaining distance between his relatively high previous offer and his lower limit at a constant or nonconstant splitting rate. If we assume a constant splitting rate of .5 or RP for the prosecutor, then the prosecutor's first counteroffer will be 8.68 *minus* .5 of the remaining distance between 8.68 and his minimum limit of 4.34, which yields a first counteroffer of 6.51 or about 6½ years.

The counteroffer process will continue until a precrossover stage is reached where if another set of counteroffers were made at the prevailing jumps (which become increasingly smaller), then that next set would involve the parties crossing over each other. At that precrossover stage, the parties are likely to split the difference at the midpoint between their last counteroffers. That midpoint or settlement sentence (symbolized S*) in our hypothetical example is at 4.72 or about 4-3/4 years. If the defendant wants to minimize his sentence, and the prosecutor wants to maximize the sentence (up to the statutory or fairness maximum), then a settlement should occur whenever ALD is greater then ALP. This is so since under that condition, the defendant-buyer is willing to pay more than the prosecutor-seller is willing to sell for, and the prosecutor-seller is willing to sell for less than the defendant-buyer is willing to pay. In the absence of any information about either side's exaggeration factor or splitting rate, we would predict the settlement sentence would be at the midpoint between ALD and ALP where ALD is greater than ALP. ALD is normally likely to be greater than ALP since if both sides perceive the payoff cells and the probability of conviction as being roughly equal, LD will be roughly similar to LP. When the defendant's bonus factor is added to LD, and the prosecutor's discount factor is subtracted from LP, then ALD is likely to be greater than ALP since both sides are likely to have larger litigation costs than settlement costs. If in the exceptional situation ALD is not greater than ALP, then negotiations are likely to break down, and the defendant will either go to trial or plead guilty without a negotiated plea depending on which of those two alternatives has the lowest expected value or likely sentence.[35]

Variations and Implications

This general model can be varied on a number of dimensions. First, some defendant-buyers may have or perceive that they have only one alternative seller from which they can buy. For example, where the judge and the prosecutor work together or think alike, then going to trial or LS_1

would be the only determinant of LD or LP. Likewise, where going to trial would cost more than pleading guilty even if the defendant were certain of an acquittal, then a non-negotiated plea or LS_2 would be the only determinant of LD or LP. If plea bargaining is not a meaningful alternative, then the defendant must choose between alternative one (trial) and alternative two (non-negotiated plea) rather than between one and two on the one hand and alternative three (negotiated plea) on the other.

A second dimension on which the model can vary is whether the defendant or the prosecutor views the probability of conviction as a point (like .5, .7, 1.0, or 0.0) or as a range (like from .2 to .6 or from 0.0 to 1.0). In our general model we worked with PC as a point. Where PC is a range it can be reduced to a point by calculating what is known as a Hurwicz optimism-pessimism coefficient for either the defendant or the prosecutor. The range is then multiplied by that coefficient, and then the product is subtracted from the top of the range to obtain a meaningful point for the defendant, or added to the bottom of the range for the prosecutor. Thus if the defendant thought PC was about .2 to .6, and he scored .75 on the Hurwicz optimism-pessimism test, then the PC point would be .6 minus 3/4 of the .4 difference between .2 and .6, which yields a PC point of .3. Similar conversion calculations can be made where the defendant or prosecutor thinks of a cell payoff as being a range rather than a point.

A third dimension on which the model can vary relates to the value of any of the givens shown at the bottom of Figure 11. One can change the value of a, b, c, d, PC, or %X for either the defendant or the prosecutor and then determine through the above calculations

(1) whether a settlement would still be likely to occur, and

(2) if so, at what sentence, and

(3) if not, whether the alternative the defendant would be likely to use would be trial or a non-negotiated plea.

In general, if both sides perceive the same increase or decrease in either the cell payoffs or the probability of conviction, then the likelihood of reaching a settlement remains constant. Anything that decreases the litigation costs of either side decreases the likelihood of a settlement, but anything that decreases the settlement costs increases the likelihood of settlement.

A fourth variation on the model is the fact that it can be either static or dynamic. A static variation would merely indicate

(1) what the defendant's maximum bargaining limit should be in light of his or her payoff matrix and nonsentence goals, and

(2) what the prosecutor's minimum bargaining limit should be in light of his payoff matrix and nonsentence goals.

Convergence would then be predicted at the midpoint between those two limits, provided ALD is greater than ALP. Otherwise, there will be no convergence. A dynamic variation of the model, however, takes as its givens the exaggeration factor and the splitting factor of the bargainers as well as their limits, and then predicts convergence at the midpoint between the last two counteroffers before they cross over, also provided that ALD is greater than ALP. The dynamic variation clearly considers more information. It not only informs each decision-maker of the optimum strategy he or she should follow in deciding whether or not to accept an offer from the other side, but it also provides some information relevant to how to proceed from the initial offer to each counteroffer until convergence is reached or until negotiations break off.[36]

By varying a hypothetical defendant or prosecutor on these dimensions, one can stage numerous scenarios in order to determine the effects on settlement outcomes due to changes in the perceptions of the parties and especially due to changes in the judicial process. These effects illustrate the causal and policy implications of the model. For example, increasing either free counsel or pretrial release decreases the likelihood of a settlement by decreasing the defendant's litigation costs. Both free counsel and pretrial release, however, also decrease the likelihood that the defendant will be forced into an artificially high settlement due to lack of counsel and the pressure of wanting to be released from pretrial incarceration. Improving the criminal discovery process (whereby both sides can obtain more information relevant to the probability of conviction and the cell payoffs) increases the likelihood of settlement by making LD closer to LP so that the defendant's bonus factor and the prosecutor's discount factor can more easily make ALD greater than ALP. Improving criminal discovery also increases the likelihood that the settlement agreed upon will be closer to the "true" sentence that would be awarded at trial in a system where judges do not give rewards for pleading guilty or punishments for exercising one's right to be tried.

The model also indicates that reducing court delay will have mixed effects on settlement likelihood and settlement outcomes. Settlement likelihood is reduced by delay reduction for those defendants who are in jail awaiting trial, since awaiting trial in jail is a substantial litigation cost that is avoided by pleading guilty and receiving probation. Settlement likelihood is, however, increased by delay reduction for those guilty defendants who are out of jail awaiting an incriminating trial, since being out of jail and then having to go in is a substantial settlement cost that is avoided by postponing the trial. Long delay may also increase the prosecutor's willingness to settle since his burden of proof becomes harder to meet and thus his litigation costs go up as his witnesses become more forgetful or disappear. The exact effect of delay thus depends on whether we are talking about a defendant in or out of jail, and whether the prosecutor is relying on evidence that has a high or low time-decay rate.

With a plea bargaining model like that described above, one can also determine in a deductive logical manner the effects on settlement of rules excluding illegally obtained evidence or other legal rules that affect negatively or positively the probability of conviction. If both the defense attorney and the prosecutor accurately perceive the lowering effect of such an exclusionary rule, both ALD and ALP will go down, but ALD will still be greater than ALP. Settlement should thus still result although at a lower level. Likewise, the model can deduce the effects of abolishing capital punishment or other system changes that affect the value of payoff cell d (such as sentence upon trial conviction) or other payoff cells. If both the defense attorney and the prosecutor accurately perceive the lowering effect of such a punishment reduction rule, both ALD and ALP will also go down, but ALD will still be greater than ALP.

So long as ALD is greater than ALP even if they are miscalculated, it is to the apparent advantage of both sides to settle somewhere between those limits. Even then, the possibility exists of a premature termination of negotiations because the defense attorney mistakenly thinks ALP is above ALD, or the prosecutor mistakenly thinks ALD is below ALP, when in reality a mutually beneficial settlement could have been reached. The possibility also exists that one side may emotionally break off negotiations, believing that the other side is not making a big enough concession, even though he knows ALD is greater than ALP. These two possibilities bring out the need to combine empirical social psychology with deductive decision theory in order to fully understand the two-person or two-group bargaining situation. Both perspectives are needed in the development of causal and optimizing theories of political science and the legal process (Simon, 1959; Edwards and Tversky, 1967).

V. CONCLUSIONS

We have now discussed the three main operations research models for arriving at decisions that will optimize some quantitatively measured goal. These models are linear programming, inventory modeling, and decision theory. One element that all three models have in common in their procedures is that they each involve two or more simultaneous equations or inequalities that intersect when graphed in such a way that the points of intersection generally represent the points toward which the behavior of an individual (or individuals) tends to move (or should move) if he wants to maximize given goals. In working with the substantive and procedural problems of the political or legal process, one may have to resort to non-precision forms of measurement in order to apply the operations research models even though those quantitative models were generally originally developed for application to easier-to-measure monetary variables. The causal and policy insights to be gained may, however, well merit the extra effort.

Those insights may prove beneficial to such policy-appliers as public administrators and trial court judges for improving their work in efficiently making decisions that will maximize social benefits without exceeding certain social costs, or that will minimize social costs without falling below a minimum level of social benefits. Those insights may also prove beneficial to such policy-makers as legislators and appellate court judges for improving their work in deciding what goals should be maximized, what costs should be minimized, what constraints should be placed on the decision-making of policy-appliers, or what alternative means should be chosen to achieve given ends particularly with regard to the effect of system changes on the decision-making of policy-appliers. In addition, the insights from operations research models may prove especially beneficial to political scientists and other researchers who are seeking

(1) a better understanding of why policy-appliers and policy-makers decide or behave the way they do, and

(2) a more meaningful role in making rational means-ends policy recommendations.

The concepts and methods of operations research enable political and social science researchers to do the kind of rational policy analysis which many such researchers have long sought to be able to do. Those concepts and methods emphasize such matters as:

(1) the measurement of goal variables or social indicators at a middle-range level of generality;

(2) the relating of policy variables and other inputs to the goal variables in the form of regression equations, production functions, or cost functions;

(3) the need for making trade-offs or mixed strategies among the policy variables given scarce available resources;

(4) the need for operating within political, legal, economic, social-psychological, and other constraints;

(5) the need for considering nonlinear diminishing returns curves and U-shaped cost curves; and

(6) the need for considering the role in reaching optimum decisions of the probability of the occurrence of key but uncertain events.

Those concepts and methods provide a number of possible gains with regard to forcing one who makes the application (or consumes the results) to be more precise and imaginative in:

(1) defining the problem,

(2) deciding what data is needed to resolve the problem,

(3) measuring the relevant alternative means variables,

(4) graphing the problem,

(5) clarifying the legal, political, and other constraints,

(6) calculating the cost and benefit relations with the alternative means variables,

(7) deciding whose goals or values should be recognized, and

(8) deriving various optimum allocations from the above considerations.

As implied above, the main thing that all three models have in common is that they are capable of provoking useful insights that might otherwise be missed by viewing political science and legal process problems only from other research perspectives. These models provide insights for comparing equilibrium or optimum behavior with empirical behavior so that one can make policy recommendations to bring the empirical closer to the optimum, or so that one can revise the values he or she attributes to the policy-makers in order to bring the alleged optimum closer to the empirical. They also provide insights for understanding the effects on other variables of changing political policies and decisions, and the effects on political policies and decisions of changing other variables. They help to clarify assumptions, goals, alternative means, payoffs from alternative means, contingent probabilities, and other elements essential to understanding more fully the basic simplicities and subtle complexities of the political, legal, and social process.

NOTES

1. For general introductory textbooks on operations research, see Richmond (1968); Baumol (1965); Theil, Boot, and Kloek (1965); and Wagner (1970).

2. On linear programming in general, see Richmond (1968: 277-405); Baumol (1965: 70-166, 270-294); and Wagner (1970: 31-134).

3. For further discussion of the problem of rationally allocating campaign expenditures, see Kramer (1966: 137-160); Agranoff (1972); and Nagel and McCarthy (1976).

4. The campaign expenditures data comes from Jennings (1974), made possible by the Federal Election Campaign Act of 1971. The expenditures for television and radio come from Federal Communications Commission (1973). The voting data comes from Scammon (1973). Who the incumbents were as of the 1972 election was determined by checking Congressional Quarterly (1971) for all districts in each state since there was redistricting between 1970 and 1972. Whether a nonincumbent candidate was a member of the out-party was determined by checking the party affiliation of the incumbent for the area in which the candidate was running. Scammon (1973) provides maps of the congressional districts for 1970 and 1972 in order to see the areas that correspond to the district numbers.

5. On doing a regression analysis between policy alternatives and goals, see Blalock (1970: 273-285) and Tufte (1974). The regression equation given above contains two policy variables or activity variables. It controls for the variable of incumbency and being a member of the in-party by virtue of how the approximately twice 435 congressional candidates were partitioned or fractionated into the above-mentioned four subsets. It controls for the variable of total votes available by using percent of the two-party vote as a dependent variable rather than absolute votes obtained. One could control for additional variables like the other candidate's expenditures by either adding those variables to the regression equation, or by using those variables to calculate a predicted %V for each of the 58 candidates, and then using predicted %V minus actual %V (rather than just actual %V) as the dependent variable with $M and $P as the independent variables. One could also control for the influence of anticipated %V on $M and $P by calculating a predicted $M and a predicted $P from another variable. Our new regression equation would then involve %V as the dependent variable and predicted $M, predicted $P, and the other variable as the independent variables. By controlling for incumbency and being a member of the in-party, however, there probably is no other variable that is likely to substantially cause anticipated %V to influence $M and $P across many of the 58 congressional campaigns.

6. When one works with the logarithms of %V, $M, and $P, then $M and $P are capable of accounting for 55% of the variation among the 58 candidates with regard to the percent of the two-party vote which they received. When one works just with %V, $M, and $P rather than their logarithms, then $M and $P are capable of accounting for 50% of the variation. This indicates that even within the limited range of those three variables, the diminishing returns perspective better fits the data although both fits are good relative to most social science relations with so few variables. The same computer routine that gives the slopes or regression weights for $M and $P also indicates what percent of the variation on %V they collectively account for.

7. The benefit maximization allocation was found by solving the pair of simultaneous equations $M + $P = $100, and

$$(.04)(27\%)(\$P)^{.12}(\$M)^{.04-1} = (.12)(27\%)(\$M)^{.04}(\$P)^{.12-1}$$

The first equation shows that all $100 should be spent. The second equation shows that the marginal rate of return or nonlinear slope for $M should equal the marginal rate of return for $P, so that nothing can be gained by shifting from one activity to the other. The cost minimization allocation was found by solving for a pair of simultaneous equations in which the first equation was

$$51\% = 27\%(TC - \$P)^{.04}(\$P)^{.12},$$

and the second equation was the same as the second equation above except TC–$P was substituted for $M. This gives two unknowns (TC and $P) and two equations which simultaneously satisfy all the constraints.

8. To ease the work involved in linear programming, there are now available many preprogrammed computer routines that only require a simple statement of the constraints to satisfy and the goals to optimize in order to calculate the optimum allocation points for two or more activity variables. Unfortunately, such computer routines are not so readily available for diminishing returns or nonlinear programming problems, but those situations can often be handled either graphically or with the aid of an electronic calculator for doing the logarithmic and exponential arithmetic involved. Computer routines for doing linear and nonlinear regression analysis are also helpful for determining the equal benefit line or curve equations.

9. For further detail on the methodological problems involved in allocating effort to civil rights activities, see Nagel and Neef (1976a).

10. Each regression coefficient indicates the marginal rate of return on equality improvement for each activity. Thus, the .32 means that if effort to fight discrimination in the schools goes up one unit on its 5-point scale, then composite equality improvement is predicted to go up about a third of a unit on its 5-point scale. Where the marginal rates of return for an activity are close to zero, one could consider them as not being significantly different from zero and therefore only allocate what the minimum constraint provides for those activities.

11. On graphing and analyzing the multiple activity allocation problem, see Richmond (1968: 370-379) and Baumol (1965: 292-279).

12. For further details concerning the substantive literature, the Auerbach data, and other aspects of the application of linear programming to the OEO legal services problem, see Nagel (1973).

13. On optimum mix allocation with nonlinear relations, see Baumol (1965: 129-147, 205-207, 266-269) and Richmond (1968: 106-122, 378-380).

14. Such an equation could be arrived at by using the logarithms of S, $L, and $C for each legal service agency in the sample in a linear regression analysis in order to obtain the numerical parameters of the equation.

15. Virtually everything you always wanted to know about calculus (applied to minimization and maximization problems) but may have been afraid to ask can be found in Baumol (1965: 42-69) and Richmond (1968: 40-66, 577).

16. On handling the multiple-activity nonlinear allocation situation through the use of partial derivatives or slopes expressed in terms of other variables besides the dependent and independent variable, see Baumol (1965: 57-59) and Richmond (1968: 78-79).

17. Another variation on linear programming (besides working with nonlinear or log-linear transformations of the relations between the goal variable and the activity variables) is the variation of integer programming. This optimizing technique is basically the same as linear programming except the activity variables are such that they cannot meaningfully attain values other than integers. An example might be determining how many people or precincts to allocate to each legislative district where those people or precinct units are not divisible. Another example is determining how

many congressmen and which ones to allocate to congressional committees (Uslaner, 1974; Shepsle, 1973).

18. For further details on the free press versus fair trial problem in both the optimum level and optimum mix contexts, see Nagel, Reinbolt, and Eimermann (1975). Free press normally includes the right of newspapers to criticize government policymakers, but in this context it only refers to the right to report damaging information about a defendant in a pending criminal case. Fair trial normally includes the right to counsel and other rights, but in this context it only refers to the right of a defendant not to be damaged by media reports concerning him and his pending trial. Thus, in this context, those variables are the complements of each other.

19. On the inventory modeling problem and the more general problem of finding the maximum point on a hill-shaped benefits curve or the minimum point on a valley-shaped cost curve, see Richmond (1968: 7-10, 53-61, 87-88) and Baumol (1965: 49-56, 65-67).

20. Bitterness costs are figured at less than lost wages on the assumption that a defendant found not guilty has his potential bitterness from having been held in jail reduced partly by his pleasure at being found not guilty and by his recognition that legitimate mistakes can be made in arresting and prosecuting.

21. For further details on the problem of optimizing the percentage of defendants to release prior to trial, see Nagel, Wice, and Neef (1976).

22. A positive convex curve slopes upward with its center pointing toward the 100% point on the graph. A negative convex curve slopes downward with its center pointing toward the zero point on the graph. A positive concave curve slopes upward with its center pointing away from the 100% point on the graph. A negative concave curve slopes downward with its center pointing away from the zero point on the graph.

23. A curve that has a quadratic form is one that can be expressed by an equation of the form

$$Y = aX^2, \quad \text{or} \quad Y = b_0 + b_1 X + b_2 X^2$$

where b_0 can equal zero, b_1 can equal 1, and b_2 equals a. A curve that has a rectangular hyperbolic form is one that can be expressed by an equation of the form $Y = ax^{-1}$, or the equivalent $Y = a/x$.

24. The bail problem can be treated as a problem in maximizing total benefits where total benefits equal total holding benefits (that is, the negative of the total releasing costs) plus total releasing benefits (that is, the negative of the total holding costs). Holding benefits are rearrest and crime committing dollars saved by not releasing defendants. Releasing benefits are jail storage, GNP, and bitterness dollars saved by not holding defendants. Likewise the bail problem can be treated as a problem in maximizing net benefits where NB = THB − THC, NB = TRB − TRC, or NB = −TRC − THC. All these interchangeable formulations produce the same %H* of 4%.

25. One can consider the %H optimization problem to be a problem in finding the optimum mix between %H and %R (that is, between the percent to hold and the percent to release) where %H + %R = 100%. Doing so algebraically involves combining the equation

$$TC = 1185(\%H)^{1.31} + 77(\%H)^{-.17}$$

and the similarly derived equation

$$TC = 61(\%R)^{-2.99} + 16(\%R)^{1.43}.$$

The combination yields

$$TC = 593(\%H)^{1.31} + 39(\%H)^{-.17} + 31(\%R)^{-2.99} + 83(\%R)^{1.43}.$$

This last equation can be used to create a series of negatively-sloping indifference curves on a two-dimensional graph with %R on the vertical axis and %H on the horizontal axis. The optimum point is thus the point on the consumption possibility line $100 = \%H + \%R$ where the highest indifference curve is reached. At that point, $\%R = 96$, and $\%H = 4$. For further detail on comparing this optimum mix perspective with the optimum level perspective that we have been using, see Nagel, Reinbolt, and Eimermann (1975).

26. If one thinks in terms of total holding benefits and total releasing benefits rather than THC and TRC, then the geometry involves concave (or bowing out) curves rather than convex ones. The THB curve is concave positive (like a typical diminishing returns curve) because as we get closer to holding 100% of the arraignees, we begin holding the best arraignees who are least likely to commit crimes or fail to show up, and therefore the holding benefits taper off. The TRB curve is concave negative (like a reverse diminishing returns curve) because as we get closer to holding zero percent of the arraignees we begin releasing the worst arraignees who are least likely to be innocent, contribute much to the GNP, or cost much in jail, and therefore the releasing benefits taper off.

27. For discussion of the applicability of the U-shaped cost minimization model to due process problems, see Tribe (1971: 1386-1389), Posner (1973), and Nagel and Neef (1976b).

28. For discussions of the applicability of the cost minimization model to regulatory severity especially in the pollution field, see Ridker (1967) and Scott (1973).

29. Some of the above distinctions with regard to arriving at cost or benefit curves are made in Hirsch (1970: 159-162, 147-183).

30. In the inventory model, the THC and TRC curves are derived as follows: THC equals UHC times the number of units held. The number of units held equals the inventory size divided by two on the assumption that over the time period, the inventory goes repeatedly from X to zero and back to X and again to zero, and $(X + 0)/2$ averages $X/2$. Thus,

$$THC = UHC(X/2)$$

which is the same as

$$THC = (UHC/2)(X)^{1}.$$

TRC or total outage cost equals the cost of having to reestablish the inventory (which is URC) multiplied by the number of times (which is Q) the inventory has to be reestablished during the period. Q equals the amount of sales during the period divided by the size of the inventory (which is X). Thus, $TRC = URC(Sales/X)$ which is the same as $TRC = (URC \cdot Sales)(X)^{-1}$.

31. On the probabilistic inventory model and expected cost calculations, see Richmond (1968: 228-250, 266-269) and Brennan (1972: 365-374).

32. For further details on the decision to release or hold prior to trial and the decision of how high the bail bond deposit should be set, see Nagel, Neef, and Schramm (1975).

33. On one-person decision theory, see Richmond (1968: 527-560); Baumol (1965: 550-568); Raiffa (1968); and Mack (1971).

34. For further detail on the plea bargaining model, see Nagel and Neef (1976c).

35. On the general two-person bargaining situation and related game theory, see Richmond (1968: 501-526); Baumol (1965: 529-549); Cross (1969); Newman (1965); and Rappaport (1966).

36. On dynamic equilibrium analysis, see Brennan (1972: 226-245 and 71-74) and Cortez, Prezewoski, and Sprague (1974).

REFERENCES

AGRANOFF, R. (1972) The New Style in Election Campaigns. Boston: Holbrook.

BARKAN, J. and J. BRUNO (1972) "Operations research in planning political campaign strategies." Operations Research 20 (Sept.-Oct.): 924-941.

BAUMOL, W. (1965) Economic Theory and Operations Research. Englewood Cliffs, N.J.: Prentice-Hall.

BLALOCK, H. (1970) Social Statistics. New York: McGraw Hill.

BRENNAN, M. (1972) Preface to Econometrics. Cincinnati: South-western.

Congressional Quarterly (1971) Dollar Politics: The Issue of Campaign Spending. Washington, D.C.: Congressional Q.

CORTEZ, F., A. PREZEWOSKI, and J. SPRAGUE (1974) System Analysis for Social Scientists. New York: Wiley.

CROSS, J. (1969) Economics of Bargaining. New York: Basic Books.

EDWARDS, W. and A. TVERSKY (1967) Decision-Making. Baltimore: Penguin.

Federal Communications Commission (1973) Report on Political Broadcasting and Cablecasting, Primary and General Election Campaigs of 1972. Washington, D.C.: F.C.C.

HIRSCH, W. (1970) The Economics of State and Local Government. New York: McGraw-Hill.

JENNINGS, J. (1971) "Quantitative models of criminal courts." Santa Monica, Calif.: Rand.

JENNINGS, W. (1974) Part II, The Annual Statistical Report of Contributions and Expenditures Made During the 1972 Election Campaigns for the U.S. House of Representatives, 93rd Congress, 2nd Session, Document 93-284. Washington, D.C.: Gov. Print. Office.

KRAMER, G. (1966) "A decision-theoretic analysis of a problem in political campaigning." Mathematical Applications in Political Science. New York: Arnold Foundation.

LAIDLAW, C. (1972) Linear Programming for Urban Development Plan Evaluation. New York: Praeger.

MACK, R. (1971) Planning on Uncertainty: Decision Making in Business and Government Administration. New York: Wiley.

MERRILL, F. and L. SCHRAGE (1969) "Efficient use of jurors: a field study and simulation model of a court system." Washington Univ. Law Q. 1969 (Spring): 151-183.

NAGEL, S. (1973) Minimizing Costs and Maximizing Benefits in Providing Legal Services to the Poor. Sage Professional Papers in Administrative and Policy Studies, vol. 1, series 03-011, Beverly Hills and London: Sage Pub.

——— and J. McCARTHY (1976) "Rationally allocating campaign and governmental expenditures among geographical districts." (Mimeographed paper available from the senior writer).

NAGEL, S. and M. NEEF (1976a) The Application of Mixed Strategies: Civil Rights and Other Multiple-Activity Policies. Sage Professional Papers in American Politics, vol. 3, series 04-029. Beverly Hills and London: Sage Pub.

——— (1976b) "Using deductive modeling to determine an optimum jury size and fraction required to convict." Washington Univ. Law Q. 1976 (Spring).

——— (1976c) "Decision theory, equilibrium models, and plea bargaining." Indiana Law J. (Summer and Autumn).

——— (1976d) "Finding an optimum geographical allocation for anti-crime dollars and other government expenditures." Political Methodology (December).

——— and S. SCHRAMM (1975) "Decision theory and the bond-setting decision in criminal cases." (mimeo) Available on request.

NAGEL, S., K. REINBOLT, and T. EIMERMANN (1975) "A linear programming approach to problems of conflicting legal values like free press versus fair trial." Rutgers J. of Computers and the Law 4: 420-461.

NAGEL, S., P. WICE, and M. NEEF (1976) The Policy Problem of Doing Too Much or Too Little: Pretrial Release as a Case in Point. Sage Professional Papers in Administrative and Policy Studies, vol. 4, series 03-037. Beverly Hill and London: Sage Pub.

NEWMAN, P. (1965) The Theory of Exchange. Englewood Cliffs, N.J.: Prentice-Hall.

PABST, W. (1973) "A study of juror utilization." LEAA, Reducing Court Delay. Washington, D.C.: Gov. Print. Office.

POSNER, R. (1973) "An economic approach to legal procedure and judicial administration." J. of Legal Studies 2: 399-458.

Programming Methods (1971) Final Report on the Development of a Criminal Court Calendar Scheduling Technique and Court Day Simulation. New York: Programming Methods, Inc.

RAIFFA, H. (1968) Decision Analysis: Introductory Lectures on Choice under Uncertainty. New York, Addison-Wesley.

RAPPAPORT, A. (1966) Two-Person Game Theory: The Essential Ideas. Ann Arbor, Mich.: U. of Michigan Press.

RICHMOND, S. (1968) Operations Research for Management Decisions. New York: Ronald Press.

RIDKER, R. (1967) Economic Costs of Air Pollution. New York: Praeger.

RUEGG, R. (1974) Life Cycle Costing of Police Patrol Cars: Summary Report. Washington, D.C.: Nat. Bur. of Standards.

SCAMMON, R. (1973) America Votes 10. Washington, D.C.: Gov. Affairs Inst. and Congressional Q.

SCOTT, D. (1973) Pollution in the Electric Power Industry. Lexington, Mass.: Lexington-Heath.

SHEPSLE, K. A. (1973) "A model of the congressional committee assignment process: constrainted maximization in an institutional setting." Presented at the 1973 annual meeting of the Amer. Pol. Sci. Assn.

SIMON, H. (1959) "Theories of decision-making in economics." Amer. Econ. Rev. 49 (June).

THEIL, H., J. BOOT, and T. KLOEK (1965) Operations Research and Quantitative Economics. N.Y.: McGraw-Hill.

TRIBE, L. (1971) "Trial by mathematics: precision and ritual in the legal process." Harvard Law Rev. 84 (April): 1329-1393.

TUFTE, E. (1974) Data Analysis for Politics and Policy. Englewood, Cliffs, N.J.: Prentice-Hall.

USLANER, E. (1974) Congressional Committee Assignments: Alternative Models for Behavior. Sage Professional Papers in American Politics, vol. 2, series 04-019. Beverly Hills and London: Sage Pub.

WAGNER, H. (1970) Principles of Management Science with Applications to Executive Decisions. Englewood Cliffs, N.J.: Prentice-Hall.

ABOUT THE AUTHORS

STUART S. NAGEL is a professor of political science at the University of Illinois and a member of the Illinois bar. He is the author with Marian Neef of *Decision Theory and the Legal Process* (1978), *Legal Policy Analysis: Finding an Optimum Level or Mix* (1977), *The Legal Process: Modeling the System* (1977). He is the author or editor of *Policy Studies and Review Annual* (1977). *Modeling the Criminal Justice System* (1977), *Policy Studies and the Social Sciences* (1975), *Policy Studies in America and Elsewhere* (1975), *Improving the Legal Process: Effects of Alternatives* (1975), *Environmental Politics* (1974), *The Rights of the Accused: In Law and Action* (1972), and *The Legal Process from a Behavioral Perspective* (1969). He has been an attorney to the Office of Economic Opportunity, Lawyer's Constitutional Defense Committee in Mississippi, National Labor Relations Board, and the U.S. Senate Judiciary Committee. Dr. Nagel has been a fellow of the Ford Foundation, Russell Sage, NSF, ACLS, SSRC, East-West Center, Illinois Law Enforcement Commission, and the Center for Advanced Study in the Behavioral Sciences. He has also been a grant recipient through the Policy Studies Organization from the Departments of Justice, Labor, HUD, Energy, Agriculture, Transportation, and HEW, and from the Rockefeller and Guggenheim Foundations.

MARIAN G. NEEF is an assistant professor of political science at City University of New York, Baruch College. In addition to the abovementioned books, she is the author with Stuart Nagel of such monographs as *Too Much or Too Little Policy: The Example of Pretrial Release* (1977); *Operations Research Methods: As Applied to Political Science and the Legal Process* (1976); and *The Application of Mixed Strategies: Civil Rights and Other Multiple-Activity Problems* (1976). She has also coauthored numerous articles in such journals as *Policy Analysis, American Bar Association Journal, Judicature, Political Methodology, Public Administration Review, Journal of Criminal Justice, Human Behavior, Journal of Legal Education, PS,* and various law reviews.

$9.75 each

Quantitative Applications in the Social Sciences

A SAGE UNIVERSITY PAPERS SERIES

SPECIAL OFFER

(for **prepaid** orders only)

Order any 10 papers for $78.00 and save $19.50

Orders under $30 must be prepaid. California residents add 7.25% sales tax. Illinois Residents add 7.75% sales tax. All prices subject to change without notice.

On prepaid orders, please add $2.00 handling charge.

SAGE PUBLICATIONS

P.O. Box 5084,
Thousand Oaks, California 91359
PHONE: (805) 499-9774
FAX: (805) 499-0871

11/94

☐ 1 Analysis of Variance, 2nd Ed. Iversen/Norpoth
☐ 2 Operations Research Methods Nagel/Neef
☐ 3 Causal Modeling, 2nd Ed. Asher
☐ 4 Tests of Significance Henkel
☐ 5 Cohort Analysis Glenn
☐ 6 Canonical Analysis and Factor Comparison Levine
☐ 7 Analysis of Nominal Data, 2nd Ed. Reynolds
☐ 8 Analysis of Ordinal Data Hildebrand/Laing/Rosenthal
☐ 9 Time Series Analysis, 2nd Ed. Ostrom
☐ 10 Ecological Inference Langbein/Lichtman
☐ 11 Multidimensional Scaling Kruskal/Wish
☐ 12 Analysis of Covariance Wildt/Ahtola
☐ 13 Introduction to Factor Analysis Kim/Mueller
☐ 14 Factor Analysis Kim/Mueller
☐ 15 Multiple Indicators Sullivan/Feldman
☐ 16 Exploratory Data Analysis Hartwig/Dearing
☐ 17 Reliability and Validity Assessment Carmines/Zeller
☐ 18 Analyzing Panel Data Markus
☐ 19 Discriminant Analysis Klecka
☐ 20 Log-Linear Models Knoke/Burke
☐ 21 Interrupted Time Series Analysis McDowall/McCleary/Meidinger/Hay
☐ 22 Applied Regression Lewis-Beck
☐ 23 Research Designs Spector
☐ 24 Unidimensional Scaling McIver/Carmines
☐ 25 Magnitude Scaling Lodge
☐ 26 Multiattribute Evaluation Edwards/Newman
☐ 27 Dynamic Modeling Huckfeldt/Kohfeld/Likens
☐ 28 Network Analysis Knoke/Kuklinski
☐ 29 Interpreting and Using Regression Achen
☐ 30 Test Item Bias Osterlind
☐ 31 Mobility Tables Hout
☐ 32 Measures of Association Liebetrau
☐ 33 Confirmatory Factor Analysis Long
☐ 34 Covariance Structure Models Long
☐ 35 Introduction to Survey Sampling Kalton
☐ 36 Achievement Testing Bejar
☐ 37 Nonrecursive Causal Models Berry
☐ 38 Matrix Algebra Namboodiri
☐ 39 Introduction to Applied Demography Rives/Serow
☐ 40 Microcomputer Methods for Social Scientists, 2nd Ed. Schrodt
☐ 41 Game Theory Zagare
☐ 42 Using Published Data Jacob
☐ 43 Bayesian Statistical Inference Iversen
☐ 44 Cluster Analysis Aldenderfer/Blashfield
☐ 45 Linear Probability, Logit, Probit Models Aldrich/Nelson
☐ 46 Event History Analysis Allison
☐ 47 Canonical Correlation Analysis Thompson
☐ 48 Models for Innovation Diffusion Mahajan/Peterson
☐ 49 Basic Content Analysis, 2nd Ed. Weber
☐ 50 Multiple Regression in Practice Berry/Feldman
☐ 51 Stochastic Parameter Regression Models Newbold/Bos
☐ 52 Using Microcomputers in Research Madron/Tate/Brookshire
☐ 53 Secondary Analysis of Survey Data Kiecolt/Nathan
☐ 54 Multivariate Analysis of Variance Bray/Maxwell

☐ 55 The Logic of Causal Order Davis
☐ 56 Introduction to Linear Goal Programming Ignizio
☐ 57 Understanding Regression Analysis Schroeder/Sjoquist/Stephan
☐ 58 Randomized Response Fox/Tracy
☐ 59 Meta-Analysis Wolf
☐ 60 Linear Programming Feiring
☐ 61 Multiple Comparisons Klockars/Sax
☐ 62 Information Theory Krippendorff
☐ 63 Survey Questions Converse/Presser
☐ 64 Latent Class Analysis McCutcheon
☐ 65 Three-Way Scaling and Clustering Arabie/Carroll/DeSarbo
☐ 66 Q-Methodology McKeown/Thomas
☐ 67 Analyzing Decision Making Louviere
☐ 68 Rasch Models for Measurement Andrich
☐ 69 Principal Components Analysis Dunteman
☐ 70 Pooled Time Series Analysis Sayrs
☐ 71 Analyzing Complex Survey Data Lee/Forthofer/Lorimor
☐ 72 Interaction Effects in Multiple Regression Jaccard/Turrisi/Wan
☐ 73 Understanding Significance Testing Mohr
☐ 74 Experimental Design and Analysis Brown/Melamed
☐ 75 Metric Scaling Weller/Romney
☐ 76 Longitudinal Research Menard
☐ 77 Expert Systems Benfer/Brent/Furbee
☐ 78 Data Theory and Dimensional Analysis Jacoby
☐ 79 Regression Diagnostics Fox
☐ 80 Computer-Assisted Interviewing Saris
☐ 81 Contextual Analysis Iversen
☐ 82 Summated Rating Scale Construction Spector
☐ 83 Central Tendency and Variability Weisberg
☐ 84 ANOVA: Repeated Measures Girden
☐ 85 Processing Data Bourque/Clark
☐ 86 Logit Modeling DeMaris
☐ 87 Analytic Mapping and Geographic Databases Garson/Biggs
☐ 88 Working with Archival Data Elder/Pavalko/Clipp
☐ 89 Multiple Comparison Procedures Toothaker
☐ 90 Nonparametric Statistics Gibbons
☐ 91 Nonparametric Measures of Association Gibbons
☐ 92 Understanding Regression Assumptions Berry
☐ 93 Regression with Dummy Variables Hardy
☐ 94 Loglinear Models with Latent Variables Hagenaars
☐ 95 Bootstrapping Mooney/Duv
☐ 96 Maximum Likelihood Estimation Eliason
☐ 97 Ordinal Log-Linear Models Ishii-Kuntz
☐ 98 Random Factors in ANOVA Jackson/Brashers
☐ 99 Univariate Tests for Time Series Models Cromwell/Labys/Terraza
☐ 100 Multivariate Tests for Time Series Models Cromwell/Hannan/Labys/Terraza
☐ 101 Interpreting Probability Models Liao
☐ 102 Typologies and Taxonomies Bailey
☐ 103 Data Analysis Lewis-Beck
☐ 104 Mult. Attr. Decision-Making Yoon/Hwang
☐ 105 Causal An. w/ Panel Data Finkel

Quantitative Applications
in the Social Sciences

A SAGE UNIVERSITY PAPERS SERIES

$9.75 each

SAGE PUBLICATIONS, INC.
P.O. BOX 5084
THOUSAND OAKS, CALIFORNIA 91359-9924

Place
Stamp
here